In his work, *Thinking Outsid[...]* think differently about missio[...] world. This book will challeng[...] leadership, reaching international students, migration, and embracing God's abundant grace through the trials and delights along life's journey!

J.D. Payne
Author, missiologist, and pastor of church multiplication,
The Church at Brook Hills, Birmingham, Alabama (USA)

What on earth is God doing sending a Twi-speaking African medical doctor to pastor an English-speaking Chinese church in French-speaking Canada, supported in part by young people from Ghana? An African proverb suggests that 'when God shuts a door, He opens a window.' While various agencies were strategizing on how to get the Good News into 'closed doors' God continued His work of breaking down old paradigms and stereotypes of making disciples of all nations. Welcome to the new paradigm of God's mosaic of mission from anywhere to everywhere, confirming that in Christ East meets West and South meets North regardless of cultural differences! Dr. Yaw Perbi's 'Yes Lord!' account of God's wonderful ways challenges us to say 'Yes Lord' to new ways the Holy Spirit is taking global mission out of old wineskin and making it sweeter day by day in spite of mitigating factors. I wholeheartedly commend this refreshing book to us!

Femi B. Adeleye, *Ph.D*
Director of Church Partnerships, World Vision International
Former Associate General Secretary, IFES

I always give thanks to God that Dr. Yaw Perbi has served at the Montreal Chinese Alliance Grace Church as our interim English pastor since 2012 until now. The Lord is doing amazing things far beyond what we could imagine.

Through Dr. Perbi's new book, *Thinking Outside the Window*, you will get to know many amazing life-changing stories through *out of the box* thinking, *out of the box* mission strategies, and *out of the box* ministries. The most precious thing is the inspiration to get *out of the box* regarding your own mission.

I highly recommend you read this book so that we all may have the same mind as Jesus Christ; seeing through the eyes of Jesus, *Thinking Outside the Window*.

Rev. Philip Cherng
Senior Pastor, Montreal Chinese Alliance Grace Church,
Montreal, Quebec (Canada)

Dr. Yaw Perbi writes from a personal and generational experience as a deeply passionate and purposeful global missions practitioner. His audience is a new growing world with no 'sending and receiving' mission boundaries! God is at work sending His global Church to take His Gospel from everywhere to everywhere!

For the emerging generation of younger leaders, Dr. Perbi's book will bring a new, challenging and insightful clarion call to respond to God's mission with a clear understanding of the significant changes in today's global mission force and fields. For the older generation, it will bring great and renewed hope for the future of global missions as the "leadership baton" passes on!

From powerful stories of personal experience, paradigm shifting insights on the strategic nature of international and university students ministry in North America, to proven evidence of God's missionary move in Africa, Asia and elsewhere, we have here a new great title on global missions that a new generation will greatly treasure, in going strategically from 'everywhere to everywhere' until... *"this Gospel of the kingdom will be preached in the whole world as a testimony to all nations, and then the end will come."* (Matthew 24:14)

Nana Yaw Offei Awuku
Lausanne International Deputy Director,
English and Portuguese-speaking Africa
Director, Field Ministries, Scripture Union Ghana

It's the passion of Dr. Yaw Perbi that is so evident as he shares his heart for what is on God's heart—the nations. Trained as a medical doctor, Yaw reveals what early on became his personal mission, "preaching the Gospel and raising younger leaders for the rest of my life ..." Enjoy learning about the unique calling on this man's life including divine guidance in which a Ghanaian moves to Canada and catches great vision for what God is doing through the global movement of peoples. Having learned to "think outside the box," the author challenges historical and conventional paradigms in helping readers to do similarly. If you'll listen up, he'll explain "what really makes theological and missiological sense"—about which he's ready to "yell, sing and dance ... to awaken, envision, engage, and resource the whole Church to optimize the most strategic Great Commission opportunities of our time!" The global presence of international students and scholars is a tremendous opportunity and Yaw provides a fresh clarion call to the Church to engage. I commend this work to those engaged in international student ministry, and to any Christ-followers willing to be challenged about the strategic nature of Gospel ministry among these future influencers.

Rev. Beau Miller
Executive Director, Association of Christians Ministering among
Internationals (ACMI)
Minister, Presbyterian Church in America (PCA)

It is seldom that I pick up a book and read it through like a fine meal. *Thinking Outside the Window* is incredibly well-written and tasty. Dr. Yaw Perbi prepared a meal for my mind, but ultimately for my heart. The stories from his life and interaction with people caused me to evaluate my effectiveness not only in ministry, but also in relationship.

Dr. Yaw Perbi has crafted a vital and strategic work of literature as it pertains to global mission and specifically the interaction with individuals as they circulate the globe. Dr. Perbi's grasp of how to shatter the paradigm of a static 10/40 Window should be considered by missiologists and missions-minded individuals from any nation. The 10/40 Window has become incredibly dynamic and interactive, and in *Thinking Outside the Window* Dr. Perbi teaches us how to become strategically engaged with it.

The Church needs to address the changing nature of the world we have been sent into. Dr. Yaw Perbi shares his story of how he wrestled with this new global reality.

Thinking Outside the Window is a crucial piece of literature as it pertains to global mission today.

Bradley D. Friesen, *D. Min*
Pastor of Global Ministries, Centre Street Church, Calgary,
Alberta (Canada)

THINKING OUTSIDE THE WINDOW

*A riveting personal transcontinental experience
of how the mission of changing the world has
changed—and why you will want to, also!*

DR. YAW PERBI

(President, International Student Ministries Canada)

Foreword by Paul Borthwick

DEDICATION

To **Anyele**

Without whom I would neither be a husband, father, nor the man of God I am today.

Without you, neither serving in Canada nor *Thinking Outside the Window* (the experience of and the book alike) would've happened.

As one who ministers around the world, I must admit I am not the easiest person to be married to. Not many women can bear the many lonely nights and single-handedly mother-fathering children; I don't know many women who can handle both homeschooling four children and running a real estate investment company simultaneously. And to do all this with loads of divine joy!

Anyele, *"Many women do noble things, but you surpass them all."* (Proverbs 31:29)

Today, I honor you.

TABLE OF CONTENTS

PART I: WHAT BOX? WHOSE BOX?
Yesterday: The mission story and my journey

**PART II: EVEN THE HEAVENS CAN'T;
LET ALONE YOUR BOX**
Today: Current realities

PART III: DON'T GET BOXED IN
Tomorrow: The future starts with you, here and now

FOREWORD

I heard of Yaw Perbi before I met him. In a variety of conversations with Ghanaian friends who knew that my home near Boston, Massachusetts was not far from Yaw's home in Montreal, Quebec, they would ask, "Have you met Dr. Yaw Perbi?" Their questions made me anticipate the day when we'd meet face-to-face.

Several years ago, that day came, and the day remains forever in my mind – but not because I was so impressed by the deep and diverse ministry of Yaw. My appreciation for Yaw, his family and his ministry came later.

The day stands in my mind because I was leading a seminar at a mission conference in Montreal. Being a bi-lingual conference, I was allowed to teach in the only language I know – English. But knowing that most of my listeners spoke both French and English, I would occasionally insert a French word or phrase here and there in an effort to make French speakers feel more welcome.

After I finished my presentation and the question-and-answer session, I stated, "Well, our seminar time is up. *Je suis finis.*" To me, my French attempt meant "I am finished" as in "the seminar is over."

But the laughter in the crowd let me know that I had made a mistake. I think it was Yaw who gently corrected me: "I think you mean to say '*J'ai finis*' as in 'I *have* finished.'"

"What did I say?" I asked.

He responded, "You told us that you are finished – as in your life is over – as in you're dead." Lesson learned. Even a sincere effort in crossing cultures can result in embarrassing mistakes!

I tell you that story because in a sense, it represents one of the biggest messages of this book. Yaw Perbi, with great stories, historical connectivity, personal anecdotes, and biblical challenges, tells us:

- Our limited view of cross-cultural missions as an 'over-there-only' vision *is finished*.
- Our wrong assumptions about the opportunities in cross-cultural outreach *is finished*.
- Our days of doing nothing as we watch people from all over the world come into our midst *are finished*.

If you, like me, are part of a people group that has been in North America for three or more generations, *Thinking Outside the Window* is a call to open our eyes, our hearts, our mouths, and our homes to the 'world that has come to us.'

If you, like Yaw, are new immigrants and new residents in North America, *Thinking Outside the Window* is a call to realize that God has sent you here – not only to reach out to other newcomers but also to serve as missionaries to the longer-term occupants of the land who look like me.

To all of us, *Thinking Outside the Window* is a call to get engaged with the world God has placed us in – reaching out across the hall in our apartment buildings, across the street in our neighborhoods, on the campus, in the workplace, across cultures and to the ends of the earth.

A Toronto pastor once observed, "God called us to go to all the nations. We didn't go, so God is bringing all the nations to us." *Thinking Outside the Window* reflects how we can be informed, involved, and obedient to God's new trans-national calling.

Thank you, Yaw, for reminding us that an old vision *is finished*. God is doing a new thing. May God help us all to get on board!

Paul Borthwick
Senior Consultant, Development Associates International
Author, *Western Christians in Global Mission: What's the Role of the North American Church?*

INTRODUCTION

I have just finished reading the draft of *Thinking Outside the Window* on the computer, and I can't wait to get a published copy in my hands so that I can use a highlighter to mark the many gems contained between its covers. What is exciting is that other readers will find their own gems related to ministry among international students and scholars that might apply to their lives and contexts.

The International Student Ministry (ISM) movement has been slowly developing in North America since the 1950s, partly because the Church has not readily caught the vision of a strikingly obvious strategic world missions opportunity and obligation in its community and on its campuses.

Since only three books on ISM have been produced to help the North American Church engage in loving and serving students from abroad, with the last being published in 1997, Dr. Yaw Perbi's contribution is not only current, but stretches forth into the future and into expanded strategic considerations for ISM. It stretches forth through recurring examples and recommendations to go beyond one's default context, or boxed-in limitations and paradigms of ministry.

It expands strategic considerations by including new topics, such as student leadership development and also support development of ISM workers, that are not usually addressed in the basic core elements of ISM training, and that comprise the three earlier books (*Building Bridges of Love*, Frank Obien,

1974; *The World at Your Doorstep*, Lawson Lau, 1984 [later upgraded under slightly modified title]; and *The World at Your Door*, Tom Phillips, W. Terry Whalin, Bob Norsworthy, 1997).

The three prior works were written in America and primarily for an American readership, though the first two authors were originally from Asia (Obien, Philippines, and Lau, Singapore). Dr. Perbi's focus is the Canadian Church and penned in Canada, though it contains frequent reference to his Ghanaian background and connections.

Yaw Perbi's approach and style are richly diverse. He declares, "I do not write this book as a scholar, a professional theologian or missiologist" since his primary audience does not need an academic treatment as such, but he communicates heart to heart, life to life. This is not a missiological textbook on ISM (as much as that is needed), but an autobiographical display of Sovereign interventions, and surprising, eye-opening discoveries of a grand and global missions opportunity delivered by God to our neighborhoods. Yaw's passionate plea is to open our doors and come out of our comfortable boxes to receive God's placement of the world's future leadership and influencers He is putting in front of us.

Like a baseball pitcher with a variety of delivery styles, Yaw utilizes powerful stories, inspiring quotes, teaching and preaching (reasoning and passion), history and name-recognition relationships, along with the fundamentals of Scripture, statistics, and sensible strategies.

In Part I you'll journey with Yaw (and his wife and children) as he witnesses and testifies of God's guidance, goodness, and grace in directing (and redirecting) his plans towards God's purposes in fulfilling the Great Commission. You'll see professional training and practice in medicine in Africa surrendered to a "full-time" missionary calling, and also pastoral ministry in a Chinese church, based in French-speaking Montreal, Canada.

Part II highlights the tremendous reality of the strategic nature and biblical basis of "diaspora missions" and international student ministry, and statistics that are applicable world-wide.

Part III introduces some new and additional exhortations for ISM, that of leadership development and engaging in partnership development, including support from abroad. The book pulls together a variety of inspirational elements and rational, strategic propositions with a call for each believer to exchange our personal ambitions for God's best plan and purpose for us.

Oh yes, some readers who do not know Yaw Perbi's personality, may initially react to his forthright declarations and transparency, and what may appear to be egocentric boasting, such as a recounting of achievements and a confident character...please be patient and finish the journey with him, and I trust you'll see that he is being a faithful witness of God's grace in his life, as he himself continues to learn and grow along the pilgrimage, like all us sheep.

Leiton Edward Chinn
Lausanne Senior Associate for ISM
Past President, Association of Christians Ministering among Internationals (ACMI)

PROLOGUE

EGO AND LOGOS

A s an *African* medical doctor pastoring an *English*-speaking *Chinese* church in a *French* city in North *America* you would suppose I certainly must know a thing or two about "thinking outside the box!"

Yet for the first few months of 2013 I struggled. I had an internal wrangling, and sometimes even wrestling with God like the patriarch Jacob, because I had been invited to serve as the president of a major ministry in Canada and I didn't want to...initially. I had valid excuses, but the bottom line was that I was too busy and egocentric.

I was not only the proud father of three young children (then 5, 3, and 1)—which in itself is a full-time job—but was serving as interim pastor at the Montreal Chinese Alliance Grace Church and was also Global CEO of The Human Development Group (The HuD Group), a holistic emerging leadership development organization.

That wasn't all. I wasn't only a busy man, I was a businessman. I was a consultant at Investors Group, a member of IGM Financial Inc., Canada's largest long-term mutual fund managers, and had over a million dollars worth of assets I had gathered in less than two years. There were times I was spending about half of my time in Toronto (a six-hour drive from Montreal) doing business and ministry and the other half in Montreal. It is no wonder that many of my friends in Canada's financial capital often asked, "Why don't you simply move to Toronto?"

But the egocentric part was that I really wanted to focus my attention on nurturing "my baby"—The HuD Group. You see, eight of my young friends and I had begun this ministry about a decade earlier in Ghana, West Africa, and now the organization had varying degrees of work in about a dozen countries. After a long two-year, laborious and cash-intensive process, we had finally been granted charitable status by the Canada Revenue Agency and I wanted to focus a lot of my attention on growing this baby of mine. Why would I serve as president of another organization, especially one that wanted to empower younger leaders too?

The Lord reminded me of some wise words a great mentor who had visited Montreal from John Maxwell's EQUIP headquarters in Atlanta in early 2010 had uttered and used them to convict me. On that visit, Doug Carter, Senior Vice President of EQUIP, had quipped: "For a long time, the Kingdom of God has not advanced as it should because of egos and logos!" Here I was, both my ego and logo getting in the way of my obedience to a divine call.

As stubborn as I was, even as of the time I was doing that four-and-a-half-hour flight from Montreal to Calgary to interview with the Board of International Student Ministries of Canada (ISMC), I couldn't care whether or not I landed the job. In that sense, I had very little pressure because I really wasn't looking for a job anyway.

Actually, I never really applied for this position per se. The outgoing president, Paul Workentine, had asked for my CV, which I emailed to him. He himself, as he later confessed to me, was quite sure I wasn't going to respond to the Board's invitation to come on board. I'm pretty sure that on that fateful February afternoon at the First Alliance Church in Calgary, the Board wondered if I wasn't a rather cocky young man, having the nerve to tell them (with all due respect), "I'm not looking for a job. I will only take on this role if I *sense strongly* that the LORD Himself is calling me to this."

Meanwhile, around the same time the Chinese congregation I was serving in Montreal was eagerly hoping I would accept *their* offer to come on board as the substantive, full-time pastor of the English congregation. Up until then, I was serving in an interim, part-time role (though I now insist there's nothing like a part-time pastor. It doesn't exist!).

In fact, one of those days, a Mandarin congregation elder met me in the basement corridor and expressed the hope that I wasn't going to leave them because he had heard from the grapevine that I was probably going to take up "this *biiig* post" nationally.

But quite frankly, the more tempting offer was the church's—because it offered a regular, reliable, stable salary (which I had never known ever since I quit practicing medicine three-and-a-half years prior). With ISMC, one had to "go and raise your own financial support" from friends, family, business people, and churches. "Wow," I thought, "who wants a job where you have to go and fetch your own salary?"

Finally, when I was made an offer by ISMC I said, "Yes;" a life-changing word. One day, in prayer, as I wrestled with the invitation from ISMC and my long-drawn response—and I can't even clearly recall whether I had finally yielded then or not—I was praying about the famous "10/40 Window" (the area between latitude 10 degrees north and 40 degrees north, which is the hardest to reach with the Gospel) when the Lord spoke clearly to me: "But Yaw, *I am thinking outside the window.*" What did He mean? Why did He say that? You're just on the verge of finding out! Even I am *still* discovering, window after window!

PART I:

WHAT BOX? WHOSE BOX?

*The voyage of discovery is not in seeking new landscapes
but in having new eyes.*
~ Marcel Proust

*We don't see things as they are,
we see things as we are.*
~ Anais Niin

~1~

ONCE UPON A WINDOW

Of boxes and paradigms

"Expect great things from God;
attempt great things for God."
~WILLIAM CAREY

A popular management term, which has now slipped into the mainstream, is "thinking outside the box." To quote the all-knowing wise old man, Wikipedia, "**Thinking outside the box** (also **thinking out of the box** or **thinking beyond the box**) is a metaphor that means to think differently, unconventionally, or from a new perspective. This phrase often refers to novel or creative thinking. The term is thought to derive from management consultants in the 1970s and 1980s challenging their clients to solve the "nine dots" puzzle, whose solution requires some lateral thinking."[1] (See diagram below.)

THE "NINE DOTS" SOLUTION

The goal of the puzzle is to link all nine dots using four straight lines or fewer, without lifting the pen and without tracing the same line more than once. One solution appears below.

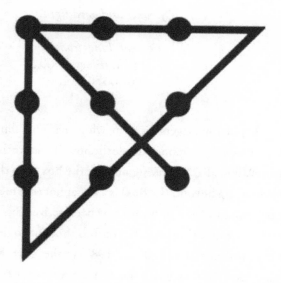

You will notice from this solution that unless one goes beyond the boundaries (literally "outside the box") to link all dots in four straight lines, one may never get to connect the dots.

"IT'S ALWAYS BEEN LIKE THIS!"

Throughout the history of the world, whenever significant progress has been made or a real breakthrough has come about, it has been because someone went beyond the conceptual framework or paradigm of his day or field. Someone refused to take "it has always been like this," "it has never been done before," or even "that is impossible" as a final answer.

Indeed, think about it: over a hundred years ago who ever heard of a human being flying? Or metal floating in the air—as heavy as it is? It must have taken some real thinking outside the box and a whole lot of guts for the Wright brothers to do what they did. Even their own father—who was a reverend minister for that matter—is said to have discouraged them. Apparently, to him, it wasn't God's will (oh, the things humans attribute to God!) for man to fly!

Out of the box, out in the wind, on December 17, 1903, Wilbur and Orville Wright made four brief flights at Kitty Hawk with their first powered aircraft. The Wright brothers had invented the first successful airplane.[2] I love the comment of Edward R. Murrow: "The Wright brothers' first flight was not reported in a single newspaper because every rookie reporter knew what could and couldn't be done."

One of the most famous "boxes" in sports was the "one-mile box." For many years, it was thought that no one could run a mile under four minutes. Sports pundits had called it an "insurmountable human limitation." The prior world record of 4:01.3 had stood unbeaten for a humiliating nine years. "It has always been like this."

One fateful day in 1954, a 25-year old young man, a medical student at that, would change that and get us all out of that 'box' forever. It was great to see Sir Roger Bannister at over 80 years old on television during the London Olympics in 2012. Roger would run that mile in three minutes and 59.4 seconds!

After the fact, now that everyone was thinking outside that limiting box, it took Bannister's rival, Australian John Landy, only forty-six days to not only repeat the under-four-minute feat but actually break the Brit's record! In a later rematch both did run the mile under four minutes and Bannister was again triumphant.[3] Indeed since then, it has become rather unthinkable that any athlete worth his salt will do any less!

When it comes to mission, "in Christianity, an organized effort for the propagation of the Christian faith,"[4] there have been a number of serious "outside the box" episodes that have significantly advanced the missionary enterprise since the days of the initial Jewish band—Philip, Peter, Paul—who first went to the Gentiles, when many of those who came to be Christ-followers before them seemed quite content in reaching only their fellow Jews. Those Christ-followers wouldn't leave the box around Jerusalem, and even Judea, for quite a while.

Careful observation of this and other phenomena reveals that first we make our boxes; then these boxes make us. They literally put dimensions on our perceived possibilities. So we make our own boxes and live in them. Fair enough if we want to continue in our 'habit' as human beings. But to put God in a box?!

We need to be careful *how* we think, how we see things—our mindsets, our paradigms. The greatest teacher that ever lived once said, "The eye is the lamp of the body. If your eyes are healthy, your whole body will be full of light. But if your eyes are unhealthy, your whole body will be full of darkness. If then the light within you is darkness, how great is that darkness!"[5] What if your paradigms are incorrect and the light in you is actually darkness?

LAUSANNE, 1974: WHO MOVED MY BOX?

I wasn't there in Lausanne, Switzerland, in 1974; in fact, I wasn't even born. But I've heard and read how way back then there were many who actually thought the work of the Great Commission, telling the whole world the good news about salvation in Jesus Christ, was done. Finito!

In fact, in 2010 I met an elderly distinguished German gentleman in South Africa who told me that he had been a missionary to this same country in the 1970s and was recalled by his mission organization in Europe to return home because the work of the Great Commission was done. Apparently, his was not the only mission organization which placed a moratorium on missions in the 1970s!

You can only imagine then how critical Billy Graham's convening of some two thousand Christian leaders to contemplate the work of the Great Commission at Lausanne, Switzerland was. This was the first International Congress on World Evangelization (ICOWE) in 1974.

There and then, the Lord used Dr. Ralph Winter to challenge the box and to re-examine the evangelical eye with which we were reading the Scriptural text regarding mission. Jesus had said, "Go and make disciples of all nations," and we had been obeying that commandment from the first century until the twentieth. Now we were done, or so we thought, because we read the text wrongly.

Indeed, while every geopolitical state must have heard the Gospel by the 1970s, what Dr. Winter pointed out at ICOWE was that the word "nations" was "panta ta ethne" in the original Greek text, which properly translates "people groups" (if you like, clans and tribes) and not the modern geopolitical countries that we had come to know.

So indeed, India as a country or geopolitical state, for example, surely has heard the Gospel and has over twenty-seven million Christian adherents. Yet, out of the 2,256 people groups in India 2,033 of them, representing 1.18 billion people, are still classified by evangelicals as "unreached" even today.[6]

According to Joshua Project, current data suggests that of the world's 7.2 billion people, there are 9,756 distinct people groups across countries (counting each distinct people group in the world only once) and 16,713 people groups by country (counting every group once for each country in which they reside).[7]

The definition used by mission strategists for *people group* is "a significantly large grouping of individuals who perceive themselves to have a common affinity for one another because of their shared language, religion, ethnicity, residence, occupation, class or caste, situation, etc., or combinations of these."[8]

Again, Joshua Project classifies three billion people as "unreached," made up of 4,083 people groups across countries (counting each distinct people group in the world only once) or 7,064 (counting each group once for each country in which they reside).[9]

An *unreached people group* is "a people group within which there is no indigenous community of believing Christians able to evangelize this people group."[10]

In the mid-1990s, mission strategists sought to quantify this definition. After considering sociological trends suggesting that two percent of a population can have a significant impact on the whole, mission leaders settled on the criteria for *unreached* as less than two percent true Christ-followers and less than five percent Christian adherents (this includes all forms of Christianity, i.e. anyone that would call themselves a "Christian").[11]

So at the first ICOWE there was this huge paradigm shift, a significant challenge to think outside the box of geopolitical states and think "ethne," people groups.

MANILA, 1989: UNTO US A BOX IS BORN!

Come the second International Congress on World Evangelization in Manila, Philippines (Lausanne II), and unto us a box is born. Luis Bush, a renowned mission strategist, literally drew a box on the world map—the area between latitude 10 and 40 degrees north—and described it as "the resistant belt." And rightly so. This area, mainly covering the middle portion of the eastern hemisphere, had had very little penetration of the Gospel and showed no indication that this was about to change. Bush highlighted the need for a major focus of evangelism there.

Incidentally, this same "resistant belt" had been described nearly eighty years earlier by Samuel Zwemer as "unoccupied fields," in his 1911 book published with the same title, delineating the Islamic, Buddhist, and Hindu areas.[12]

According to Wikipedia, "In 1990, Luis' research led to a meeting with the developer of the first PC based GIS software. They analyzed the region using a box between 10 and 40 degrees north latitude and called it the *10/40 Box*. A few weeks later, Luis' wife Doris recommended renaming it the *10/40 Window*, stating that this region ought to be seen as a "window of opportunity.""[13]

This box has served Christians in general, but missionaries in partic-ular, very well in many ways over the past quarter of a century. It also has had its critics, especially considering generalizations such as "this region has the poorest of the poor," yet having nations like South Korea and Japan in the mix.

But by and large, the 10/40 Window has come to stay in Christian parlance. Yet this very 10/40 "box" is what the Lord said to me that *He* is thinking outside of. But even before He told me this in 2013—the third (Lausanne) International Congress on World Evangelization had taken place only three years prior—and there had been another paradigm shift there! This time, I was there in person, to see and hear with my own eyes and ears.

~2~

AFRICANS OR CHINESE?

Forget the box—the mission has changed!

"The New Testament writers were not scholars who had the leisure to research the evidence before they put pen to paper. Rather, they wrote in the context of an 'emergency situation,' of a church which, because of its missionary encounter with the world, was forced to theologize."
~MARTIN KÄHLER

I do not write this book as a scholar, a professional theologian, or missiologist. Like Apostle John and other writers whom Martin Kähler so aptly describes above, for me, too, "That which was from the beginning, which we have heard, which we have seen with our eyes, which we have looked at and our hands have touched—this we proclaim concerning the Word of life."[14]

When I do presentations on global missions, there's almost always a particular introductory slide I love to put up and ask: "Are these Chinese or

Africans?" In that box (picture frame) is a group of three African children in glamorous Chinese outfits.

I later explain to my audience that those are my three little (then) African-Canadian children in Chinese garb, celebrating the Chinese New Year in February 2013. Of course, every year we celebrate with our fellow Chinese Christians who, because of a combination of the Gregorian and lunar-solar calendars don't get to start their new year until late January or even mid-February. How come? What has the Chinese calendar, clothes, or church got to do with my African family?

Well, like they say in North America, "wake up and smell the coffee!" The mission has changed ... *seriously!* The above illustration has come about because for the past few years God decided to choose an *African* to pastor an *English*-speaking, *Chinese* church in a *French* city in North *America!* I'm not even sure if that is "outside the box!" There's no box!

CAPE TOWN, 2010: NO BOX, NO MORE!

The first time it really seriously hit me how the global mission has significantly changed was at Lausanne III—the third International Conference on World Evangelization held in Cape Town in 2010.

I wasn't born when Lausanne I was held; I couldn't have been at Lausanne II either, but thank God Almighty, I was in Cape Town among some 4,200 Christian leaders from 198 countries.

Cape Town, 2010 has been called by some, like *Christianity Today,* as "the most representative gathering of Christian leaders in the two thousand year history of the Christian movement."[15] And the most resounding call to the Body of Christ I repetitively heard in South Africa was, "the mission has changed!" The mission is no longer "from the West to the rest," as has been the pattern in the past few hundred years. The box is gone. The mission is now God's people everywhere taking the Gospel everywhere.

In fact, the exact words used to characterize this phenomenon were these: "the center of gravity of Christianity has shifted." And people still speak of that. In unison, at the 10th Assembly of the World Council of Churches in Busan, South Korea, Kenneth Ross, co-author of *The Atlas of Global Christianity* stated: "This 100-year shift between 1910 to 2010 of the center of gravity is the most dramatic in all of Christian history."[16]

It was in Cape Town that this shift really made its mark on me. Come to think of it, the fact that the conference was even held on African soil in the first place (and in hitherto *apartheid* South Africa for that matter!) should've been evidence enough for me that the mission has indeed changed.

Etched in *The Cape Town Commitment*, the conference communique compiled after the historic global Church gathering, were these words: "At least two thirds of the world's Christians now live in the continents of the global south and east. The composition of our Cape Town Congress reflected this enormous shift in world Christianity in the century since the Edinburgh Missionary Conference in 1910. We rejoice in the amazing growth of the Church in Africa, and we rejoice that our African sisters and brothers in Christ hosted this Congress."[17]

Ross, who happens to be Council Secretary at the Church of Scotland World Mission Council as well, also uses 1910 as his gauge because in that year in Edinburgh, Scotland, the first modern ecumenical missions conference was held—and there was not even one African present! No, not one! In fact, Africa was classified among "the heathen" to be reached.

"Less than 10 percent were Christians in 1910 but that's nearly 50 percent today. In sub-Saharan Africa that's well over 70 percent. In absolute terms, the number of Christians in Africa has risen from 12 million in 1910 to almost 500 million today,"[18] Ross further states.

"While Europe's share of the world's Christians has fallen dramatically from 66 percent in 1910 to just over 25 percent in 2010, Africa's share has rocketed from a mere two percent to 21.6 percent during that period of time."

"Since 1981, Southern Christians are once again in the majority [the Global South had majority of Christians for the first 900 years of Christianity]. The Christian faith is on the march in the Global South."

Similarly, "There are now parts of Asia with a significant Christian presence and that was absent in 1910. A hundred years ago there were 25 million Christians in Asia. Today, that figure is 358 million."[19]

EVERYWHERE TO EVERYWHERE

For me, this is not about who is in the majority or not; this is not even about "balance of power," or "the re-emergence of the South," or any of that. It's about the fact that the mission is now, more than ever, God's people everywhere taking God's Word everywhere.

Perhaps if my own Chinese church had had this knowledge and a clear understanding of it earlier, the English assembly wouldn't have gone fifteen years without a pastor, all because they were looking for someone who looked Chinese!

Today the mission has changed. It is no longer people from the west going east, or the northern hemisphere going south; the mission is now God's people everywhere going everywhere. So you have Brazilians preaching the Gospel in Portugal; Chinese missionaries in Israel; the biggest congregations in Europe are pastored by Africans (including one in Ukraine which is almost 100 percent Ukrainian, led by the Nigerian pastor Sunday Adelaja). I recently heard of Korean missionaries reaching out to First Nations (Aboriginal peoples) in Canada. There you go!

I serve as the pastor of a Chinese church. Intrigued, people ask when they hear this: "Are you Chinese?" My answer is, "Of course, can't you see?" pointing to my Nubian face. And then I add in jest, "And don't forget my name is Yaw—Yao Ming, that's my brother!"

On a more serious note, this phenomenon is a microcosm of a bigger *shift* in world missions that God Himself has orchestrated in these last days.

On a recent short-term mission trip to Ghana with two of the Chinese-Canadian young people from my congregation, we experienced the joy and wonder of worshipping with a Chinese congregation in Accra, which is partly led by a Swiss couple who used to be missionaries in China, now serving the Chinese in Ghana!

Today, there are Chinese targeting Israel for missions (the Back to Jerusalem movement), Indonesians planting churches in Holland, Nigerians reaching America and Kenyans re-evangelizing England. God's mission is more than ever from everywhere to everywhere. Hallelujah!

Recently one young mentee of mine from Ghana, who had gone to spend considerable time in France preaching the Gospel, wrote to me desiring some direction regarding the tug in his heart to serve as a long-term missionary to France. I connected Ernest to Phil Bauman, the SIM Ghana director who actually happens to be Canadian and has become a good friend of mine.

It turned out in the end that SIM decided to take on Ernest as a Ghanaian missionary intern and prepare him to be sent from SIM Ghana as a missionary to France. It has been a long, not-straight-forward process because there apparently was no precedent. SIM in Ghana would normally not be a missionary-sending agency to Europe, but guess what? God is on the move everywhere to send His people everywhere!

THE NUMBERS TELL A STORY

The first time I met Jason Mandryk was at that pivotal Lausanne Younger Leaders Gathering 2006 in Malaysia. Even back then, though a younger leader himself, Jason was already working with Patrick Johnstone of *Operation World* fame. For a long time Jason had sensed that God was putting in him a global calling (beyond his native North America) to see the big picture, analyze global trends, and call the global Church to appropriate action.

At the time of writing, Jason actually heads *Operation World*. And this is his observation: "Nearly every country is a missionary-sending country. What used to happen 'from the West to the rest' is now an extensive and expanding global activity. Missionary vision is alive even in those countries where the church is young, small or under persecution."[20]

J.D. Payne, author of the remarkable *Strangers Next Door*, is another great tool in God's hand calling the global Church to "wake up" and see what the Lord is doing in missions today. I had the privilege of meeting and interacting with him at a Missio Nexus conference in Toronto in June 2014, the day before taking the first mission team from my Chinese-Canadian church on an African mission.

Following an email from Jason Mandryk to J.D. Payne in March 2012, the latter slightly modified the following table (from the seventh edition of *Operation World*) which tells the story of missionaries really being from everywhere to everywhere, more than I could ever shout it loud enough.

Select Countries Sending More Than Five hundred Missionaries[21]

COUNTRY	MISSIONARIES
United States	93,500
India	82,950
China, PRC	20,000
South Korea	19,950
Nigeria	6,644

COUNTRY	MISSIONARIES
United Kingdom	6,405
Canada	5,200
Philippines	4,500
Australia	3,193
Germany	3,144
Indonesia	3,000
Ghana	2,000
Netherlands	2,000
Brazil	1,976
Switzerland	1,712
Ukraine	1,599
New Zealand	1,200
Finland	908
Sweden	873
Mexico	794

COUNTRY	MISSIONARIES
Singapore	693
Norway	610
Spain	512
Bangladesh	500

THINKING OUTSIDE THE ETHNIC WINDOW

With the God-orchestrated changing trends cited above should come another significant change in the thinking of missionaries from the Global South. Many such missionaries, when they arrive at their Western destinations, tend to minister only to their kind. Chinese start Chinese churches, Koreans pastor Koreans, Nigerians lead Nigerians (at best with a few other African nationalities sprinkled in the congregation).

Every time I get to preach at a Ghanaian church in the Bronx, New York, for example (and I've preached several times to four different *denominations*), I marvel at how strategically located these churches are in the midst of some of the hardest socioeconomic and spiritually-deprived enclaves in America, and yet these Latinos or African-Americans or Anglos are bypassed every Sunday by these Ghanaians to enter a sanctuary full of fellow Ghanaians, totally in a world of our own.

I have preached almost to the point of a nose bleed, trying to get African pastors in North America to realize that the Lord brought them here to stir up the wider Body of Christ, especially the now spiritually cold Caucasian, and not just "reach their own," so-to-speak. A handful of bishops/general overseers I've had bilateral talks with humbly acknowledged this and pledged to work with their missionary-pastors on doing something concrete about it.

Since having the privilege of being among the inner circle of a dynamic Chinese congregation, I have realized the admirable missionary drive of Chinese congregations (including mine) but the pattern tends to be this: my Chinese congregants do go to France on a mission (which is a great thing since France is in dire need of re-evangelization) but they *only* go to reach out to the *Chinese* in France; when they go to Germany they do the same— reach the *Chinese* in Frankfurt or Dortmund or wherever!

While that has been a tendency of many ethnic churches, including the one I pastor, I thank God that things are shifting. The English congregation of my church has a vision to not only serve the second and third generation *Chinese* Christians in Montreal (who are mainly Francophone and Anglophone; some are even tri-lingual), but to reflect the demographics of the very multi-ethnic city in which we live. Having a Black pastor in itself is a great testament to that!

Our vision statement therefore, since I've led the congregation, has been to see a *"dynamic, grounded, intimate, **multi-ethnic community of Christ-followers** significantly serving each other and positively influencing Montreal and beyond with the whole Gospel of Jesus Christ for God's glory."* The last time I checked, our congregation was made up of eleven different nationalities/ethnicities—Hong Kong, Taiwan, Peoples Republic of China, Ghana, Nigeria, Cameroon, French Canada, Vietnam, Thailand, Trinidad and Tobago, Philippines—although we're still predominantly Chinese. Of course almost all of them are Canadian citizens.

This is avant-garde and so out-of-the-ethnic-window. So help us God, because when it works right, it *really* works!

EVEN THE QUEBECOIS

It gives me joy to no end to find that the Lord is using an African-led Chinese church in Canada to reach the largest unreached people group, not just in North America, but the entire Western hemisphere: the seven million Quebecois! That is so "outside the box!" No box, even!

At the Montreal Chinese Alliance Grace Church's last summer camp in late August 2014, I had the precious privilege and inexpressible joy of seeing Cedrik don his white gown and get baptized in Rond Lake in Sainte-Adèle, the very heart of the Laurentians.

Readying Cedrik for baptism in the Rond Lake at the camp site in Sainte-Adele, 70km from Montreal.

Cedrick Thibert is Quebecois through and through. He started attending our English service at the Chinese church through a Chinese young lady from mainland China who straddles China and Canada. The rest, as they say, is history.

And he's not the only Quebecois in my congregation. Oh, how my heart rejoices whenever I set eyes on Michel as I preach. I have had the joy and privilege of discipling this fifty-something-year-old Quebecois who has finally come to see the true light of the Gospel now. He was baptized at our Chinese church in December, 2014.

Guess what drew Michel to church. This "white man" started coming to church because of a Chinese lady he befriended, Jeng Ye Hong (Jenny). They had been friends since December, 2013. Michel even traveled from Quebec all the way to China to visit her family.

On some evenings as I disciple him via Skype, I can't help but wonder: isn't there something wrong with this picture? How did this African boy get to have this privilege?!

As if that were not enough, I had the singular honor of marrying them on January 11, 2015. The story has just begun.

What Gerrie ter Haar finds true of Europe, is equally true for many of us African immigrant pastors in North America and elsewhere in the world as well: "African church leaders in Europe are today convinced of their mission to bring the Gospel back to those who originally provided them with it. For many African Christians, therefore, migration to Europe is not just an economic necessity, but also seen as a God-given opportunity to evangelize among those whom they believe to have gone astray."[22] Personally, it is all about the latter, not at all about the former, as you will soon discover from the next chapter.

J.D. Payne, author of *Strangers Next Door*, and who himself pastors a church in Alabama, admits, "The Lord has allowed the Gospel to penetrate large numbers in the Majority World so that they may now assist us in reaching the post-Christianized countries in which we live." And *together*, the whole Church, east and west, north and south, can be a force to reckon with, sending the Gospel to the ends of the earth!

I love the slogan of the Lausanne Movement: "the *whole* Church taking the *whole* Gospel to the *whole* world" (emphasis mine).

Indeed, the mission is so much now God's people everywhere taking the Gospel everywhere, that my question really in that famous PowerPoint slide with the picture of my Quebec-born children should rather be: Are these Africans, Chinese, Quebecois-Canadians, or just Christians?[23] You tell me!

~3~

HE SAID "GO!"

Out of the box

"If you don't get out of the box you were raised in,
you won't understand how much bigger the world is."
~ANGELINA JOLIE

"To know the will of God,
we need an open Bible and an open map."
~WILLIAM CAREY

I come from Ghana in West Africa. Unlike a lot of people who want to migrate from Africa to find greener pastures elsewhere, I had a different leaning, actually, the very opposite passion. I so wanted to *stay* in Africa.

In fact, I was on a mission to *prove* to people that you can make it in Africa without leaving the continent for apparent greener pastures in the West. My conviction was this strong because "the same Lord is Lord of all and richly blesses all who call on him,"[24] and God is no respecter of persons.

He shows no favoritism or partiality, "but in every nation anyone who fears him and does what is right is acceptable to him."[25] And I was right about this truth, as I shall later share about significant financial support coming from Africa to our mission in Canada. But I was so much on this path, to the exclusion of everything else.

AMBASSADORIAL DAYS

In 1995, 1996, and 1997 I traveled to the United States (from Ghana) for various purposes. Several people encouraged me to remain in the States but I always firmly said, "No, I am going back to Africa." There was even someone who said, "Oh, but America needs talented people like you."

I retorted, "Africa needs me more." I found it so intriguing that even Americans thought I was crazy for not wanting to come and partake of their apparently 'better life.'

I had been one of four representatives of my high school in Ghana, Achimota School, to Ballard High School in Kentucky in the spring of 1995. At a visit to the University of Louisville I was even given application forms which I never bothered to fill—I believe I still have the forms tucked somewhere among my 'worldly goods.'

In 1996 I was privileged to travel to many countries, again including the United States, and Canada too, as a World Vision Youth Ambassador (WVYA). In 1997 I was back in the States, this time as a staff intern with the WVYA program.

I remember, as if it were yesterday, engaging in serious conversation with an impressionable young African who was a WVYA. This fellow teenager (late teens) was a sorry sight as he battled the numerous voices putting immense pressure on him not to make the mistake of returning to the Horn of Africa, whence he came, now that Providence had brought him to America!

These friends and relatives of his in the United States were literally saying, "just vanish" after the program was done. I was only a teen myself also, but I gave him strong advice to the contrary, not only for legal and moral reasons but my African sentiments and belief in our continent were *that* strong. He took my advice; he returned home. Today he's legally back in the US, having pursued a PhD, among other things, and is lecturing there.

I vividly recall having an interview with CNN in 1996 at the John F. Kennedy Center for the Performing Arts, Washington D.C., as a World Vision Youth Ambassador. I remember the guy who did the interview being so impressed with my oratory skills and demeanor and literally offering me an opening, "Would you want a job with CNN?"

I did not even need to think twice. I immediately responded with a big, "No!" Of course not. "I'm going back to Ghana!"

LIFE IS GOOD!

So I did go back home, did eight years of university (including medical school), and came out of my near-decade old cocoon in 2005 a metamorphosed young man alright: new doctor, new car, and new apartment. I've heard it quipped that *if you see a guy open a car door for a girl it means one of two things: either the girl is new or the car is new.* Guess what? I had both! I had a gorgeous new wife and a brand new mint green Chevrolet Optra. Life was good! I was even hosting a national TV program and had access to the president of the Republic—life was great!

And then...

DICKSON DECLARATION

Six weeks after my wedding, I found myself at a Lausanne Younger Leaders Gathering in Malaysia among 550 other emerging leaders from 112 countries. I was minding my own business at the conference in Port Dickson, near Kuala Lumpur, when the LORD so clearly spoke to me and said: "It's my world! And I send you wherever I want you!" What?! That changed everything. It literally rocked my world. That deeply shifted something in the core of my being; I began to *be transformed by the renewing of my mind.* I just knew these living words were the preamble of something; something significant was about to happen. What could it be? This was September 2006.

ACCRA ADDENDUM

At the beginning of January 2008, my wife and I were reading the Scriptures in our cozy two-bedroom apartment at Adenta, a suburb of Accra, when Genesis Chapter 12 literally jumped off the pages! God clearly said, "Leave your country, your people and your father's household and go to the land I will show you."[26] This erupted in our spirits like a volcano. It was an unmistakable call.

I remember telling my wife, "Honey, by the end of the year we will not be in this country." What I did not know was where, how, and exactly when, but I just knew in my spirit that God was about to eject us from Ghana for His greater global purposes.

ONE MAN, THREE COUNTRIES

And truly, by June I found myself in the next country, Côte d'Ivoire, because the "Ivory Coast" was in civil war and the United Nations had been asked to go and keep peace. Even though I was a civilian doctor working with the military, I was actually under the purview of the Ministry of Defense, not the Ministry of Health. And in the case of a shortage of actual military doctors, people like me were conscripted, trained, and given an honorary rank to go and do 'military stuff.'

So Dr. Yaw Perbi metamorphosed again into Captain (Dr.) Yaw Perbi and embarked with Ghanmed 5 on a chartered United Nations flight to work with the United Nations staff and peacekeepers of UNOCI—United Nations Operation in Côte d'Ivoire.

By July, barely a month later, God had also kicked my wife out of Ghana to be in Montreal, Canada to pursue her Master's in Economics at McGill University. Wow! So after all my chorus of "I'm not going anywhere," and "I'm *never* going anywhere," all of a sudden I found myself in three countries: I was slugging it out in Côte d'Ivoire, my wife was studying in Canada, and our son was toddling in Ghana with my parents-in-law. Oh, wow!

Just to give you an idea how stubborn my wife and I were about going nowhere but staying in Ghana, let me let you in on a significant secret. My wife is actually Canadian by birth. She's a 'second generation international student,' so to speak. She was born in Hamilton, Ontario when her father was doing *his* PhD at McMaster University.

If you are of Western heritage, you probably have no idea what it means to the average African who wields a Western passport! It means the world to many. I even know of people who let their wives or daughters fly out to North America when they conceive just so that their children will be "made in the USA" or born Canadian citizens.

Yet Anyele, quite as mad as her certifiably crazy husband, and totally disinterested in living in the West, never used that Canadian passport to even visit Canada, since the family returned to Ghana when she was two, right after her dad had completed his PhD studies. Of course, that quick return in itself was crazy too, especially since his wife was already several months pregnant and Ghana was in very bad socioeconomic shape. So fast-forward to the next insane generation: two crazy, pro-Africans had met and married! Anyele never stepped foot again in Canada from 1985 until twenty-three years later, in 2008, when God said, "Go!"

LEAVING IT ALL?

Going was hard on many fronts. I figure God had to do something as drastic as throw a *rhema* (profound revelatory Word of God) at us to get us out of our comfort zone.

After hands-on experience as a House Officer and Senior House Officer in the departments of surgery, pediatrics, obstetrics and gynecology, and internal medicine, I had graduated into a bonafide Medical Officer. I was specially detailed by the Commanding Officer at the 37 Military Hospital to administer the newly-started military polyclinic, solely taking care of the health needs of serving soldiers (Air Force, Army, Navy) and ex-servicemen. Their families and the general public were served by the other wings of the hospital.

Anyele and I were (and still are) both very strong believers in Ghana and always encouraged the young people to strive to make it *in* Ghana. We believed that success came from above, not abroad. We had set out to prove this, and thus far our lives were ample evidence of young, successful 'home-made' people.

In many of the two to three hundred speaking engagements I was doing each year—from business concerns through schools to churches—this theme would either be overtly spoken or implied. Through our company, NEOparadigms Ltd., we even began an "I believe in God and Ghana" T-shirt campaign. We targeted a select few prominent leaders in society and delivered to them these black T-shirts that had the words above inscribed on the back. On the front was a huge red-gold-and-green Ghana flag (the black lodestar smack in the center) with the letters G-H-A-N-A acrostically arraigned to graphically communicate the acronym: **G**od **H**as **A** **N**ation **A**head.

And there were a number of awards along the way, prodding me on. I'll only mention a couple. One was this "POS Distinct Youth Honour." On the night of December 19, 2005, in the presence of Hon. Prof. Christopher

Ameyaw Ekumfi (then Minister for Harbors and Railways), the Chief Justice of the Republic of Ghana, the President of the National House of Chiefs and other distinguished Ghanaians, the POS Foundation in collaboration with the Ministry of Manpower, Youth and Employment conferred the title 'POS' (Perfector of Sentiments), *"to appreciate your momentous role in the development of Ghana. You are noted and admired for who you are and your excellent achievement for the publication of motivational books which serve as challenges to the Youth."*

Then there was, in the following year, the Newmont Ghana Highest Achievement Award, presented to me by the Vice-President of the Republic of Ghana at the Youth Achievers Awards 2006 held by the Millennium Excellence Awards Foundation in Accra. This honor on August 19, 2006 at the Great Hall of the University of Ghana, and in the presence of several ministers of state, members of the diplomatic corps and other dignitaries, came exactly one week after Anyele and I got married.

It is not often one is inexplicably called into the office of the 2IC (soldier slang for 'Second-in-Command') in a military setting and returns grinning from ear to ear. Well, this time Gp. Capt. Nii Laryea had had me summoned to his office...but only to congratulate me on the award.

Among several media interviews and congratulatory messages from distinguished Ghanaians like the then CEO of the Ghana Chamber of Mines, Ms. Joyce Aryee, was a special congratulatory letter dated September 28, 2006 from the late Hon. Minister of Health, Maj. (Rtd.) Courage Quashigah. Portions of the honorable minister's letter, copied to my 2IC, read:

> *I write to personally congratulate you for being a recipient of the Highest Award for Excellence at the recent Newmont Ghana National Youth Achievers 2006 Awards...*
> *We in the health sector are very proud of you and urge you to continue to be an **Outstanding Achiever** even in this era of heightened indiscipline among the youth of this country.*

It is my hope that you will bring your charisma and devotion to bear on every youth you encounter and they in turn will emulate your leadership example.

On behalf of the entire health sector and on my own behalf, please accept my congratulations.

By now, hopefully, you get a sense of the pig-headedness of this newly-married, successful, *very* Ghanaian young man. So to hear the Lord say, "It is my world and I send you wherever I want you" just the next month was not as easy to take as it sounds today. And to follow up sixteen months later with, "Leave your country, your people and your father's household and go to the land I will show you;" that simply did it for me! *I* had to die.

~4~

DEATH DAY

My box is crashed and windows smashed

"God allows us to experience the low points of life in order to teach us lessons
we could not learn in any other way."
~C.S. LEWIS

E veryone has a birthday, but no one knows their 'death day.' And just as
well, because death is something many of us would rather not enter-
tain in our thoughts, especially in my traditional African context. But I
began to experience how quite universal the uneasiness around the subject
is, even in North America, as a consultant financial-advisor with Investors
Group. I was amazed that even in Canada not many wanted to deal with
risk management issues as far as insurance was concerned. Thinking about
'life insurance' made one face the 'morbid fact' that we are mortal and that
that moment will inevitably come someday.

Almost everyone remembers and celebrates their birthday. I do, too. But I also celebrate my 'death day.' I consider Monday, July 21, 2008 my 'death day.' Not only was there death in the air, death did place its proverbial icy hands on two of my compatriots. I, too, died.

But for that day and death, I doubt I would be where I am now, *thinking outside the window* and challenging you to do same! That 'death day' catapulted me on the trajectory I am on now.

"YOU'RE A FOOL!"

In May 2008, it was Gp. Capt.[27] Nii Laryea who literally pulled me out of the military polyclinic to attend an Advanced Trauma Management training by a specialized team from the United States.

This 2IC of the 37 Military Hospital was notorious for enticing, sometimes coercing, people to sign up for United Nations peacekeeping missions. By 'people,' I'm basically referring to the more stubborn civilian medics since the 'men and women in uniform' literally had no say when and where they were posted. I remember one friend of mine, a major, lamenting that he had spent only approximately two years with his wife and two sons over the last five years! For me, one more reason for being *in* the military world but not *of* it.

Several times Gp. Capt. had tried to convince me to go on a peacekeeping mission. I would always find a witty response and shrug it off. One day he couldn't hide his frank opinion. He literally said I was a fool for not wanting to go, at least to pocket some UN dollars for the sake of my young and growing family. Then again, this was the same young family I would have to leave behind for months in order to fetch those greenbacks, right?

If ever I gave serious thought to any mission, it was to Lebanon—just so that I would have the joy of visiting the Holy Land, Israel, close by and get to experience its sights and sounds. A pilgrimage of sorts, treading where the Master walked.

Of all the UN missions available, for me the least likely I would ever sign up for would be the Ivorian one, for the simple reason that it was the only one which required a year's commitment. A *whole* year! All the other missions were six months long (or should I say "short"?).

So when I was pulled out (like a bad tooth) from my regular work at the polyclinic and asked to attend this comprehensive Africa Contingency Operations and Training Assistance (ACOTA) program with a bunch of medics and paramedic trainers from the United States, not in my wildest thoughts did I consider that this could be a trap. Apart from a handful of us, 90 percent of those taking the course were there to undergo pre-mission training—the United Nations Operation in Côte d'Ivoire (UNOCI).

The Commanding Officer (CO) of UNOCI Ghanmed 5 (the fifth annual medical mission from the Ghana medical corps as part of the UN set up in Côte d'Ivoire), then Lt. Col. (Dr.) Samuel K. Adjei, and his deputy, Maj. (Dr.) Archer, as well as a host of others began trying to persuade me to join them. Wrong crowd, bad company. "Lord, please get me outta here!"

Their plea was not only sincere but dire, since the team's departure was imminent, due to leave in barely a couple of weeks, but seriously incapacitated because they still did not have a physician to travel with (they had all the other positions, including that of a surgeon, filled).

My last rotation as a Senior House Officer was in the department of medicine and I was now in charge of running the military polyclinic. I seemed the perfect fit. Like Jonah, I did a good job of running...but not for long.

Some way, somehow, I found myself in uniform, from UN blue beret to shiny black ankle-high combat boots, three-studded rank of captain on both shoulders, civilian-turned-officer in a couple of weeks, marching on the tarmac of the Kotoka International Airport on June 30, 2008, Bouake-bound.

DEATH ROW ON DEATH ROAD

People on death row know they are waiting in line. They even know when death is imminent. But how can one ever tell that a highway they've plied before, maybe even several times, that day may be their death road?

My team was stationed in the rebel stronghold city of Bouake, just about in the middle of the country (though considered 'north'). Bouake is the second most populous city in Côte d'Ivoire after the commercial capital, Abidjan. This is where the Force Nouvelles (euphemism for 'rebels') were headquartered.

It was exactly three weeks to the day we landed (Monday, June 30 to Monday, July 21) when I got on death road, unknowingly.

At approximately five minutes to nine o'clock (0855hrs GMT) on Monday, July 21, 2008, a team of three set off from UNOCI Ghanmed 5 Level II Hospital in a white, UN-inscribed Toyota vehicle en route to Abidjan. Staff Sergeant Wisdom Dogbevia was the driver and sitting with him in the front was Maj. (Dr.) Isaac Archer, our Deputy Commanding Officer (DCO). I sat on the second row of the van, basically because the latter had placed his bag on the first seat. He had insisted I could move it and sit there but I humbly declined. I had no idea that that long seat in the van right behind them was death row, literally.

We whispered a short prayer (I was the unofficial chaplain of Ghanmed 5) and had a smooth journey all the way to Yamoussoukro, where we stopped to refuel at a Total filling station. Yamoussoukoro, world-famous for its Notre-Dame de la Paix Basilica, is actually the official political and administrative capital city of Côte d'Ivoire, while the economic capital of the country is Abidjan. We could see the majestic edifice on the skyline strongly beckoning us to come tour, but no, we were men on a mission. We continued our hitherto enjoyable journey, savoring the scenery, sleeping some (of course not the driver!) and having great intermittent conversations spiced with laughter.

After about two hours the DCO ordered that we halt for each of us to disembark and take a water break (not input; output!), thus we did take a short break, approximately five minutes, to do so and continued our journey.

Throughout the journey I had drifted in and out of slumber. While on the motorway, approximately 60km from Abidjan, I was startled during my last nap only to open my eyes to see the *horrific sight* of a vehicle speedily somersaulting across the island (the bush separating the two dual carriage ways) from the Abidjan—Yamoussoukro direction and landing (no, still rolling) *right in front of our van*, barely 100 meters ahead of us! Colliding with it was imminent and inevitable—traveling at around 100 kilometers per hour, there was no way we could stop or swerve—I just knew we had had it! *Bang*!!! It was such an incredible *bang* as the metal of both vehicles with great momentum crushed into each other! It was about a quarter to one p.m. (1245hrs).

THE AFTERSHOCK

I had shut my eyes in prayer and hope, split seconds before the crash, only to realize when I opened my eyes, that we were in a total wreck, but I was *miraculously alive* and still on my feet, albeit crouched, clutching the seat ahead of me for dear life! Upon realizing my spirit wasn't leaving my body yet, I quickly checked for broken bones, for with that level of impact that should be a logical consequence. None seemed broken. I had a deep laceration on my upper left arm with pieces of broken glass stuck in there and a few other cuts, but that seemed to be it.

All of this was in a few split seconds. I quickly noticed that the driver was exhibiting signs of life, dangling over the steering wheel, so I hopped out of the shattered window on my side and opened his door. I shouted to the few locals around (who had started to gather but were rather not readily helpful) to aid me in getting him out of his seat. It was quite a task since his lower limbs were quite firmly caught between the steering wheel and the seat. We finally managed to get him stretched out beside the road.

I then quickly ran to the other side to assist Dr. Archer, only to realize he was already dead. He hung almost upside down with a totally severed right arm, completely disarticulated from the shoulder joint with blood still dripping and strewn across his face. Besides, the lower half of his body was so tightly trapped under the wreckage that it was impossible to drag him out.

Though my medical instincts in triaging told me to just leave him and find a way to transport the living S/Sgt. to a health facility, I also felt it was a gross shame to leave a military officer in such a position. I took a quick photograph of his state with my phone, an old Palm, as evidence that it was actually *impossible* to evacuate him. Within that short span of time I also managed to get a photo of the number plate of the vehicle that rammed into us and the phone number of the driver who, by the way, virtually slipped out of his car 'without a scratch' though he was apparently shaken by the incident. He gave his name as Zadi and added his phone number.

One dead; two injured. What a shock!

MORE AFTERSHOCKS

After struggling to get a willing transporter—several commuters had turned us down, only slowing down and staring at us like caged animals in a zoo—a pick-up truck with quite a load in its bucket covered by tarpaulin gave us a ride. With some help we managed to haul S/Sgt. Dogbevia onto the load and I lay beside him, praying with him. Another local hopped into the back with us (after helping us pick up a couple of bags and documents we could readily reach) and helped me shade the poor soldier's eyes and face from the scorching sun with a sheet of newspaper since he was lying supine, but his arms had no power in them.

I suspected he had a spinal injury because, not only was he unable to move his upper and lower limps, but also anytime there was a bump on the road he would complain bitterly about severe neck pain though he lay flat on his back and his neck was quite immobilized manually (as much as we could improvise). Just a moment ago he was the chief among our drivers, and now he was a quadriplegic?! My! The 'short' journey to the C.H.U. de Yopougon hospital in Abidjan was the longest sixty kilometers I have ever traveled—we seemed never to arrive!

On the way I managed to phone Ghanmed 5 Command in Bouake and informed them about the tragic incident, but due to the inconsistent phone signals along the route we could not communicate continually or give full details. They, however, managed to kick-start the UN emergency mechanisms, and by the time we had spent about forty-five minutes at the Yopougon hospital in Abidjan, the UN medical team had arrived to check on us. I still remain grateful to this day.

The UNOCI medical team, led by Jordanian Dr. Raj, reached us at the Yopougon hospital and transported us via an ambulance to a UN Level III facility in Abidjan. Later in the evening after suturing my arm and neck, I was discharged at about 2200hrs. S/Sgt. Dogbevia, I was told, was to be operated on and kept at the Intensive Care Unit (ICU). Three days later he was evacuated by air to Ghana; within two weeks, he, too, was dead.

MY CONSOLATION TODAY

While recuperating myself, I was deeply saddened when I heard the news about S/Sgt. Dogbevia's passing. Yet at the same time I had such a profound relief that he was going to spend eternity with a Christ he had apparently shunned all his life but had just received into his heart at the last minute.

This driver would typically drop off the rest of us at church and go his merry way to have his own good time elsewhere—even picking us up later than he should. This was so unbecoming of an "other rank" soldier that a couple of the Lieutenant-Colonels (officers) had been talking about court-marshaling him a few days before the accident.

On our way to the hospital, both of us bruised, bleeding and in shock and pain, I sensed the Holy Spirit of God gently whisper: "Speak to him now; speak to him now. Now is the time of salvation." I'm glad I obeyed, despite the discomfort of the present. After quickly sharing what the good news of salvation in Jesus Christ is all about, the S/Sgt. prayed with me to accept Jesus into his life as his Savior and Lord.

I was so sure he was going to live—and he did; but two weeks was not exactly what I had in mind. Today he is living forever with Jesus Christ and I will see him one day, I trust. His end is so much like the story of the thief on the cross who at the very last moment, in his dying moment, committed his life to Christ. "Today, you will be with me in paradise,"[28] was Jesus' assurance. So it is for the fallen soldier.

As far as I know, my colleague-doctor did not have a similar opportunity. Salvation is a gift, and no wonder it can only be received as a present *in* the present. Not yesterday; not tomorrow. For God says, "At just the right time, I heard you. On the day of salvation, I helped you." Indeed, the "right time" is now. Today is the day of salvation."[29]

We must do the work of God while it is day; "for night will come when no one can work."[30] And what is this work, one may ask? Jesus answers thus, "The work of God is this: to believe in the one he has sent."[31]

I NO LONGER LIVE

I did a report to the UN Provost Marshall (Military Police) that was investigating the case. I remember stating: "Considering the tragic nature of this accident and the grave extent of the wreckage, it is nothing short of a MIRACLE BY GOD that any of us survived at all to tell the tale. I am eternally grateful to God for sparing TWO of the three lives (UNOCI staff) on board!"

At that time, it was a miracle enough that two of us survived. You can imagine how much more of one it is today when in the end, of the three UNOCI staff, *only one survived* to tell the story you're reading.

But really that day I died, too. I have always loved Paul's words to the Galatians in the second chapter of his letter to that congregation, but it has taken on a completely new meaning for me now. It's so real. "I have been crucified with Christ and I no longer live but Christ lives in me. The life I live in the body I live by faith in the son of God who loved me and gave himself for me."[32]

Something beyond my box crashing (indeed the UN van was mangled like a card box) and windows smashing happened that day. To say July 21, 2008, was a defining moment for me is an understatement. You see, all the while I had *sort of* balanced medicine and ministry[33] but I just *knew* at that moment that God had spared me for a purpose—and for a purpose *beyond* just medicine. And so I said, "Lord, when this UN contract is done, I'm done. I want to spend the rest of my life preaching the eternal Gospel of Jesus Christ and raising younger leaders!" And that is what I have done since I returned to Ghana the following year and hung up my stethoscope. And like they say, "the rest is history."

LIFE COMES FROM DEATH

I have had umpteen opportunities to share the story of God's great deliverance from this fatal car crash in Côte d'Ivoire in multiple countries and contexts around the world. Oh! If only the devil knew! Hundreds have committed their lives to Christ (either for the first time, as a rededication or consecration for His service) over the years.

I *love* my ministry to younger leaders, especially international students! How else would I get to freely share my testimony and the glorious Gospel of salvation with this hijab-donning, second year PhD, electrical engineering student from Iran at the University of Calgary?

Remember my "2IC"? If you're a fool for not listening to your earthly commander, then what shall we call one who does not listen to *the* Commanding Officer of Heaven and Earth and all that exists, visible and invisible?

My Death Day became my new birth day. I was *born again,* again! Now, it's all beginning to add up.

CONNECTING THE DOTS

Only when you look back

"Life can only be understood backwards;
but it must be lived forwards."
~SOREN KIERKEGAARD

D id you ever do "dot to dot" exercises? You probably did in kindergarten. At first glance, the sequence of numbered dots on a sheet of
paper is total 'nonsense' until one trusts and obeys the teacher (or parent)
to follow the simple instruction of drawing a continuous line from dot to
dot. Sooner or later, voilà! An object is revealed. An incredible image one
could not have possibly imagined lay hidden in the maze of these seemingly
random black dots.

When we grow up and get to do 'real life' we are much less trusting. For
some of us, it takes a lot to even believe that we are not just living day-to-day,
scampering from life event to life event, but that everything and every season

is part of a bigger, grander picture, most of which we don't see until we much later look back on life.

I really never thought living outside Ghana was even an option, and frigid French Canada of all places, for that matter! Yet God's really got the end in mind—but most of us see that only when we look back, IF we will.

"GO BACK TO GHANA!"

I remember the serious mix of emotions when the KLM flight, after a long ten-hour transit at Schiphol airport in Amsterdam from Accra, was about to touch down in Montreal. It was August 20, 2009. How could I ever forget?

What had happened was that while rounding up my Ivorian mission in June 2009, Anyele was also simultaneously finishing up her Master's in Montreal but... but... she had gotten admission into a PhD program as well. Since PhDs take 'forever' to complete, it was quite obvious that if we were going to keep our relatively new family together and strong (especially after being apart for nearly a year in three different countries), our now-nearly-two-year-old first child, Nana Agyina, and I would have to relocate to Canada to join Anyele. We packed up all our worldly goods from our apartment, sent the bulk of it to our parents' for storage, and downsized our entire lives into four suitcases en route to Montreal.

Meanwhile I had already resigned from the 37 Military Hospital in July, after a very interesting exit interview with the Commander then, Brigadier-General Wadwhani. My resignation had nothing to do with Canada—I had already resolved after my 'Death Day' how I wanted to spend the rest of my loaned life; my God-given 'extra time.' I wasn't just leaving this hospital, I was leaving behind my entire medical career! This wasn't about joining the exodus of African doctors from the continent to practice in the diaspora, it was about preaching the Gospel and raising younger leaders for the rest of my life, no stethoscope attached!

Staying in Ghana, or at least Africa, to accomplish this mission with the rest of my days would've been my first choice when I had been alive to my own ways and plans. But now I was dead to self and alive to Christ's command. "Go to a land I will show you" now meant the difference between two ends of the thermometer: my Africa and Anyele's Canada.

"Stupid! What have I done? I've left everything and everyone in Africa... for what?!" I didn't say much, though. I was only musing to myself—or was I hearing voices? Anyele, Agyina and I were physically tired and emotionally tense after we arrived in our 'new country.' Even what should've been a simple discussion and decision about getting pizza for dinner almost went bazooka!

In the midst of that little tiff, and feeling like I deserved better treatment than I had received for all *my* sacrifices, I, with a sense of entitlement, remember saying to Anyele, "Look, I've left *everything* to follow *you* here."

Her response then, I must say to date, has been the most prophetic words she's ever uttered in all our married years. She retorted, "If it's because of me you have come here, then you should go back." For soon she would graduate with her Master's in Economics, do a year of PhD work and, under strange circumstances, crash out of the program.

Indeed, if she were the *real* reason I came to Canada, then I shouldn't still be here, as I will soon reveal in this chapter. In the midst of the heat, she had angrily pronounced words that would guide me for the five to six years that we've been in this country: "If you think I'm the reason you came here, then feel free to go back!" Ouch!

Errrm...let me explain what she *really* meant. Translation: "You didn't follow me here; I'm not the reason you've come to Canada. God brought you here for His greater purposes, far beyond me and a PhD." Indeed, anyone who looks at our lives today will never be able to tell that the 'human reason' we moved to Canada was Anyele. From all indications it would seem *she* rather followed me here.

BE STILL?

I still didn't know exactly how I would be carrying out my God-wired purpose in Canada, except that I knew all I wanted was to spend the rest of my life preaching the Gospel and raising younger leaders (thanks to the Côte d'Ivoire catastrophe). The most logical thing to do then was to continue my itinerant preaching (which I had already been doing back in Ghana and Côte d'Ivoire) and to establish the Canadian and global operations of The HuD Group so we could keep raising emerging leaders worldwide. We always knew, right from inception, that God was going to take this organization worldwide. In fact, the first name I gave it when I founded it was "WannaBe Inc. Worldwide." Well, world, here we are.

Was that it, was that all though? Several times I thought there should be more; I was capable of much more. Almost every time God would say, "Be still." If you know me in person—and one professor and mentor of mine in London, England calls me "peripatetic"—then you will know that this is a hard thing to ask of me!

My medical job in Africa was lucrative. I was getting double pay: first from the UN in Côte d'Ivoire and then from the military hospital in Accra by the government of Ghana. Not to mention my many entrepreneurial side gigs. Now I had quit and moved to Canada, 'jobless.' Yet it's amazing how, within the first three months of parting with my profitable profession, I made more money from itinerant preaching in Canada and the United States than I would've practicing medicine in Ghana or Côte d'Ivoire. This was an encouraging start. But I wanted to do more, be more, learn more, and earn more! The clear response of the LORD almost always still seemed to be, "Be still and know that I am God."

MIRACLES GALORE

My first six months in Canada were still on a visitor's visa because my long-awaited permanent resident status was still being processed, and yet we couldn't just hang around in Ghana—Anyele had to get back to school for the fall semester. And we had been married by "remote control" for far too long (or should I say "wifi"?).

Meanwhile there were many acts of God that clearly showed us He was with us, even in this 'strange land.' One that I will never forget is how the Canadian center in Accra processing my permanent resident status all of a sudden asked for a police report from war-torn Côte d'Ivoire—because I had lived and served there for a year. Wow! How was I going to get that from Montreal?

All attempts at getting my many UN contacts to procure this document failed. So did my father's high level contacts through his KPMG colleagues in Abidjan. Everything pointed to the fact that I had to travel all the way back across the Atlantic to Côte d'Ivoire *in person*. "Such inconvenience and waste of time," I thought. "And who was going to pay for this, anyway?" Don't forget, I hadn't seen a regular salary in five months!

Miraculously, at about that same time, in December 2009, I was due to return to Accra en route to Ibadan, Nigeria, for the final and graduating session of my two-year Africa Leadership Initiative (ALI) Fellowship. This meant the Fellowship was taking care of my plane fare! Praise the Lord!

So right after getting to Accra and attending the session in Ibadan, I got Kingsley Kwayisi (COO of The HuD Group Ghana, then, and my usual West Africa missions partner) to jump into my father's rugged military green Nissan Patrol and take the day-long drive along the southern coast of Ghana across the border into Cote d'Ivoire and further north to Bouake.

How we managed to get the police in Abidjan to detail two plainclothes investigators to travel with us on the four-hour stretch to Bouake is another story. Over there they interviewed a host of people to ascertain my conduct while I had been there.

Needless to say, I secured the Ivorian police report, handed it in to the Canadian immigration authorities in Accra and returned to Canada, by God's grace.

STILL MORE MIRACLES

I still took the risk of returning to Canada on the same visitor's visa, knowing full well that it had about a month to go before expiring, yet there was no guarantee as to when the permanent resident process would be done and an immigrant visa issued.

Just before the visitor's visa would expire, the permanent resident visa was ready. That was both exciting and excruciating at the same time because it had been barely a month since I returned from Ghana, and I knew there was no way I was going to be able to afford to fly back to Ghana only for my passport to be stamped with this new immigrant visa and then return to a Canadian port of entry as a permanent resident—not a visitor.

Again, some way, somehow, the Lord granted such favor before someone at the Canadian High Commission in Accra, who voluntarily offered a brilliant suggestion of sending my passport to the high commission by courier. She would ensure that the IM-1 visa was duly stamped in the passport and re-couriered back to me in Montreal. Wow!

And that is exactly what happened.

HE'S GOT IT ALL FIGURED OUT

While I was trying to figure out the best way, now that I had my passport in hand, to get out of the country and re-enter as an immigrant in a most cost-effective way, the Lord had it already figured out. Yes, that one, too!

You see, in January of 2010, John Maxwell's Christian leadership training outfit called EQUIP was now breaking ground in Quebec, with a maiden whole Saturday seminar in Montreal. I was very familiar with EQUIP and had not only attended training sessions in Accra, but had been a trainer myself since 2004.

Lorie Hartshorn, the EQUIP Canada leader then, put together a pre-event dinner for Montreal ministry and marketplace leaders at a nice restaurant downtown—my wife and I got invited that Friday night. Somehow.

Don't forget we're trying to connect the dots here—to see how God had always had the end in mind, way before I had any clue what He was doing! It was at this dinner that I first met Rev. Philip Cherng, Senior Pastor of the Montreal Chinese Alliance Grace Church (MCAGC), and his dynamic wife Dorothy.

At the end of the seminar the next day, I was quite convinced in my spirit that The HuD Group should formally sign a partnership with EQUIP and that meant I was to fly to Atlanta, Georgia, (where EQUIP is head-quartered) to go through their Square One training program for would-be trainers and partners and sign the partnership agreement.

I did—and on my return trip from the U.S. on February 19, 2010, I re-entered as an official permanent resident, killing two *big* birds with one *small* stone!

GRACE UPON GRACE

Oh, and that's not all. Rev. Cherng and Dorothy happened to be at Square One in Atlanta, too! They got excited about leadership training sessions I was about to hold in Montreal for younger leaders and greatly encouraged an elder and some of their youth to attend.

They had such a good time that the next thing I knew, I was being invited to conduct a similar training for all the youth and young adults at

MCAGC. Before I could say "Jack Robinson," I was being invited to preach there on Sundays from time to time.

Before I knew it, preaching at MCAGC had become a regular, monthly feature. And soon, Rev. Cherng wouldn't even fix the quarter's program without asking me which Sundays I would be available to speak!

I guess I shouldn't have been surprised when in early 2011 I was specifically invited to serve as the substantive English pastor of the church. Unfortunately, I had to decline because they wanted a full-time person and I was not ready to do that. I was still enjoying itinerant ministry and running leadership training sessions of The HuD Group. Training trips to Liberia, Sierra Leone, Ghana, Côte d'Ivoire, Gambia, Kenya, and Uganda were all in the works! Besides, we had committed to helping a fledgling Baptist church in Montreal—incidentally also called "Grace"—to get established as a multiethnic community of believers; not just Ghanaian.

After about a year, early 2012, MCAGC came back to me with a softer proposition—they were now willing that I take on an interim pastoral role, on a part-time basis. Incidentally, right about then, "the Baptist experiment" had gone under and so I officially took on the role as the African pastor of a Chinese church in June 2012.

IT GETS EVEN BETTER: TAKE ONE

How on earth did ISMC come into the picture then? Hmm... *"As for God, his way is perfect."*[34] I was just looking through my stuff while writing this portion of the book and realized that when I filled out my workshop evaluation form for International Student Ministries Canada, I never turned it in! Curiously, after checking the box that said "This workshop challenged me to get involved with this mission or one similar" I had scribbled on top of the "get involved" phrase the following word: "MAYBE."

This was November 6, 2010, at Missions Globales, usually held at the Collège Jean-De-Brébeuf, Montreal's version of the annual "Missionfests" held across the country. That day Anyele and I had attended this ISMC workshop conducted by then-president Paul Workentine and long-time Calgary staff, Angie Moline.

Of course being internationals ourselves, having a family history of international students in North America and Europe, and knowing loads of friends and family who were international students and scholars, this workshop really intrigued us. We've even done crazy things like driving six hours all the way from Montreal to Toronto just to pick up one international student arriving from Ghana!

I don't recollect anything significant happening with our ISMC connection at Missions Globales 2010. At that time our interest was much piqued but we were disappointed that there was no one in the city to *lead* this ministry—and we weren't about to start and/or lead it. We were too busy also, right? So nothing really happened with that. Not yet.

TAKE TWO!

The following year, Paul was back at Missions Globales, just as he had faithfully done yearly for nearly a decade, even without seeing any visible fruit yet. God bless him! He's a good man!

Now connecting the dots, neither of us could've imagined then that Missions Globales 2011, the event that *really* connected us on a personal level, would be the last one to be held for a long time. [At the time of writing this book Missions Globales had still ceased in Montreal.]

By this time, The HuD Group had now been formally registered and was acknowledged as a bona fide Canadian charity, and so we also officially registered to be part of the mission organizations exhibiting at Missions Globales. And you know what God did in His great sense of humor? Of all the many floor levels and wide spaces in the entire venue, He juxtaposed the booths of the two ministries: ISMC and The HuD Group.

Of course we had no choice but to talk...a lot, and visit with each other...a whole lot. So Paul strolls to our booth and sees all these leadership syllabi and workbooks The HuD Group has on display and says something like, "Oh wow! This is good stuff. As ISMC we know we're supposed to be training these international students as leaders but haven't found a specific syllabus, structure or process to do that, and it seems that is what you have." Right there and then we began to think possibilities.

When Missions Globales was over, Paul and I had a follow-up meeting at the library of Peoples Church of Montreal before he drove off to Ontario for other business. This time, it seemed like we would have some kind of formal partnership between The HuD Group and ISMC; and maybe I would come on board as associate staff of ISMC? We'll see.

In due time I even received application forms from the candidate director then, Reg Ewert, but somehow the process stalled. In fact, somehow I just couldn't bring myself to fill out those forms. There seemed to be an invisible barrier...Was that the Lord, because He had something else in mind for ISMC and me?

I ONCE WAS THEM

In the summer of 2015 my family and I had a most unusual experience of embarking on a road trip with three generations in one minivan: my parents, my wife and I, and our four children. While we left mom and dad in some places in the United States to travel elsewhere on other business, by the time we made it back home to Montreal we had clocked over 9,000km across three Canadian provinces and 13 USA states.

One of the major highlights of this once-in-a-lifetime trip was all three generations getting to go back to Louisville, Kentucky to visit my dear host family there when I was an international (exchange) student *twenty years* back! With a lot of my emphasis today on tertiary international students, I hadn't even realized till that summer that I had almost missed the fact that—albeit at the high school level and only for a month—I had myself been through the joys and sorrows of being an international student in North America!

When I first came to Ballard High School and was hosted by the Johnson family, I came *alone* as 'just a student.' Two decades later I returned to pay homage with *seven* other people spanning *three* generations and as a physician, pastor and president of an international student ministry. I was once like those I serve today. Only God knows who they too are becoming.

Thank you George and Judy Johnson (also my host brother Derek) and thanks to all those kind-hearted and faithful host families, homestays and friendship partners across North America!

SEVERAL MORE DOTS

When I think back, there are several more dots that I could connect to what and where I am in life and ministry now.

My parents' love for hosting people in our home, especially international students and scholars (from my academic mother's world) and expatriates (from my dad's business world) must have been preparation for the hospitality we also now offer internationals in our own home and within ISMC nationwide.

When I volunteered to help American students from the State University of New York (SUNY) at Brockport to get to know Accra and familiarize themselves with the University of Ghana in my late teens, did I really know I was being prepared for such a time as this? No, sir!

In a recent email exchange with the leader of the Ghana Fellowship of Evangelical Students ('Intervarsity' in Ghana, so-to-speak) we were discussing how they could be more intentional about ministering to the thousands of international students on Ghanaian university/college campuses at the moment when he suggested an "Akwaaba"[35] night.

I smiled and shook my head in disbelief because some fifteen years ago I had been involved in organizing the first-ever such welcome night (with Ghanaian food and cultural display) for international students at the drama studio of the University of Ghana. Now I'm connecting the dots and thinking, have I come full circle or what?

MUST HAVE BEEN THAT ALTAR CALL

In my medical school days I served as president of the Christian Medical Fellowship (CMF) in my penultimate year. My team and I put together an epoch joint CMF conference with our counterparts at the other major medical school in Kumasi, a 270km-drive north into the country.

Our main speaker was Rev. Dr. Solomon Aryeetey, who himself is an alumnus of our medical school and had been a medical missionary with Pioneers-Africa for decades. Let me pause and share a bit about him and Pioneers-Africa because he is one of the forerunners of God's Global South missionary thrust in our day:

> It all began in the spring of 1986, when Dr. Solomon Aryeetey, a Ghanaian medical doctor and his wife Leticia—a lawyer—were about to fulfill their "dream" of emigrating to the USA and furthering their professional careers. However, God had other plans, and He used Harold Stevens, a PIONEERS mission advocate to challenge them about the needs of the Fulani people in Mali, West Africa, and the Aryeeteys knew God was calling them to go. For seven years, they lived in the desert amongst the nomadic people, learning the language and sharing the Gospel from hut-to-hut through mobile medical clinics. During this time, they faced many hardships, including being separated from their six children. Over

time, believers were discipled and a church was started, which continues strong to this day.

In 1994, the Aryeeteys founded Pioneers-Africa to awaken and mobilize the Church in Africa to proclaim Christ to unreached people groups. Today, the Mission has over 130 African missionaries serving in places of greatest need and least opportunity of hearing the Gospel.[36]

This was a dangerous man to invite to address medical students on mission! On the final day, a Sunday, Uncle Solo (as my contemporaries and I affectionately call him) made an altar call—not the usual ones for people to give their lives to Christ for salvation. This was an altar call to give one's life to *mission*, Christ's mission. I made the "mistake" of going forward. I guess God took me seriously.

I had totally forgotten about this until I thought I was already done *connecting the dots* in this chapter when the Lord brought it to mind. I came back to insert this significant dot, shaking my head.

"I REMEMBER YOU"

It was in the spring of 1995 that I became an international student at Ballard High School, Louisville, Kentucky. The following year our family hosted an African-American exchange student, Dietrich, from Ballard, at our home in Legon, Accra. Even a couple of years later—and I had been out of high school for at least two years—I still volunteered to drive around with the students from Ballard to tour parts of Ghana.

When in 1996 I had the privilege of being a World Vision Youth Ambassador—studying, living, singing and touring with fifty young people from fifty different countries—I had NO IDEA that as a young eighteen-year old the LORD was preparing me to deal with international students from all over the world who had come to North America. That year we toured Taiwan, the USA, Mexico, and Canada.

When I joined ISMC and discovered that the British Columbia regional director then, Bert Kamphuis, had a 'tradition' of getting a dozen or so international students and a couple of staff into a van and driving across British Columbia and Alberta, singing and sharing in various churches, it was déjà vu for me—this is WVYA re-lived!

And how come the following year, 1997, I was one of only two youth ambassadors (of the fifty-one) invited back to serve as a staff intern? The other was Claudia Lopez from Colombia. I had the joy of reconnecting with her in Toronto in 2012, when she had just moved to Canada with her family. And guess who appeared at the launch of ISMC's President Circle in Toronto in February, 2014: Willie Boake, our WVYA Project Director!

In the fall of 2013, while on a western Canada tour in my first year as ISMC president, I got so excited visiting Vancouver because it was the first time I was seeing the Pacific Ocean in sixteen years! On my final Saturday morning when I was speaking at a pancake breakfast meeting in Richmond Hill, I cursorily made reference to my World Vision Youth Ambassador experience a decade-and-a-half years back when, to my utter surprise, an oriental-looking lady said to me during one of the breaks: "I remember you."

"What?" I thought.

Would you believe that this Japanese-American woman was in 1996 working for World Vision at their Seattle office and was part of the team that organized hosting us? She even still has a copy of the framed group picture we presented to her as a gift! Talk about connecting the dots!

EVEN BEFORE A DOT

And to think the first dot to be connected was actually *before* my wife was a dot of blood in her mother's womb: *"I knew you before I formed you in your mother's womb. Before you were born I set you apart and appointed you as my prophet to the nations.*"[37]

One day my father-in-law had come to visit us in Montreal for a couple of weeks. Because I had been invited to speak to a multi-ethnic fellowship at the Ottawa mega church called *The Met*, I went along with him and the whole family.

During the two-hour road trip from Montreal to Ottawa, Dr. Sowa and I continued our father-son chat—he was sitting beside me in the front seat of our minivan.

Come to think of it, I hope I never physically left my mouth opened ajar like a fool, but certainly I was shocked as he revealed the details of how he came to Canada first to pursue his Master's in Economics at Queen's University in Kingston and the circumstances under which he moved to Hamilton to continue his PhD at McMaster.

I sat in the driver's seat in awe when he explained how often he had deferred his admission, on account of family and financial issues. God knew exactly when Anyele had to be born and where—1982 in Canada—to make His purposes of using us to reach internationals in Canada today possible.

Would you believe that neither Anyele's older or younger brother is Canadian? In fact, when her dad decided to return to Ghana to serve his motherland, immediately after his PhD, Anyele was two years old and his wife Norah was six months pregnant with their third (and last) child—why wasn't he also born in Canada?

As for God, His way is perfect[38] indeed. I almost get goose bumps just thinking of and connecting these dots!

A MODERN PROPHET

I can understand some of the reasons why people do not believe that the gift of prophecy is still relevant and operational today, but I feel sorry for them. My good friend, mentor and the writer of the foreword to this book,

Paul Borthwick, comments on how "many of us in the North American church are what used to be called *cessationists*: people who believe that the gifts of miracles, signs and wonders were only for the first century."[39] Then he throws in a word of advice: "if you want to be a cessationist, don't travel! The church in the Majority World did not get the memo."[40] Indeed!

Brace yourself for a modern-day word of prophecy. You know, none of these Canadian dots regarding my wife and her family's life journey crossed my mind until one day, when we had been married several years, I remembered a prophecy I once received. The prophecy had mentioned traveling to Canada, actually Ontario, and the Lord giving me a wife in the same breath.

I know I must have been sleepy at three a.m. that Saturday morning of the prophecy, but thank God it was recorded. You see, a couple of friends and I from the Christian Medical Fellowship (CMF) had just ended our regular Friday night meetings. This was in my medical school days.

That night we were so spiritually pumped up and we wanted so much more of God's presence. So we decided to drive off campus to attend a Friday all-night prayer service being run by Prophet Atsu Manasseh at his Watered Garden church in Accra. I had become familiar with this servant of God because from time to time we would invite him to our CMF meetings to minister.

After the preaching of the Word and much prayer and singing (yeah! in Africa we do that for hours; I miss that!), Rev. Manasseh began to release a series of prophecies. It was way into the wee hours of the next morning when I heard the Spirit of the Lord speak into my future. This was June 28, 2003. Among other things He said,

> *"You will be traveling to Ontario for conference.*
> *God Himself will choose a woman for you."*

So here we are, the Ontario-born woman re-sent to Canada after twenty-three years in Ghana, during which she got married to me, for such a time as this because God knew before we were formed *in utero* that He was setting us apart and appointing us as His prophets to the nations. Guess what? The nations have come to Canada!

THE MORNING AFTER

Is it a mere coincidence that the Sunday after our wedding, the morning after, of all topics in the world, the sermon was on missions? The very bearded Uncle Jude Hama, the general director of the Scripture Union of Ghana then, in his characteristic apostolic style delivered a challenge to all and sundry to "go into all the world and make disciples." Little did we know, *little did we know...*

P.S.

Still "connecting the dots," one morning after I had already written and reviewed this chapter, a phrase from our family mission statement hit me hard during my time of morning prayer. Anyele and I knit together our "Perbi Family Mission Statement" during our honeymoon, way before we ever had children or owned a home or left our motherland.

It just struck me in a very profound way that we were prophets too: we are now living a "self-fulfilling prophecy," if you like. The last-but-one paragraph of our family mission statement reads: "This is a missionary family— receiving, raising, sending and supporting carriers of the Gospel of Jesus Christ." What we did not know was that we would be raised by God as missionaries *ourselves*, beyond receiving, sending and supporting other such individuals!

We live forwards and connect the dots backwards indeed; but we serve a sovereign God who declares the end from the beginning. "I make known the end from the beginning, from ancient times, what is still to come. I say, 'My purpose will stand, and I will do all that I please.'"[41]

So here we are in Canada, right in the midst of God's next chapter in global mission history: international student ministry.[42]

PART II:

EVEN THE HEAVENS CAN'T; LET ALONE YOUR BOX

Behold, heaven and the highest heaven cannot contain you;
how much less this house that I have built!
~ KING SOLOMON
(1 Kings 8:27, ESV)

But who is able to build him a house, since heaven, even highest heaven,
cannot contain him?
Who am I to build a house for him?
~ KING SOLOMON
(2 Chronicles 2:6, ESV)

~6~

"God is on the Move!"

In, on, over, under, around, through, and beyond boxes—even no boxes

*"God is on the move, and we can drift away from Him just by standing still.
Don't get left behind at this critical, thrilling juncture in world history.
The world can be reached in this generation."*
~William Lane Craig

*"We must be global Christians with a global vision
because our God is a global God."*
~John Stott

Y ou can't put God in a box. Dream not. Dare not. And He will do *any-thing* and *everything* within His perfect and holy character to fulfill His purposes—even if it means yanking a promising young African medical doctor from his field and folks to lead His charge, *Missio Dei,* in the world. After all, He did not even spare His own Son, but gave Him up freely for us all!

"Who has stirred up one from the east [as far east from Canada as Ghana, ten thousand kilometers east!], calling him in righteousness to his service? He hands nations over to him... [you will soon understand] I took you from the ends of the earth, from its farthest corners I called you. I said, 'You are my servant'; I have chosen you and have not rejected you."[43] God is on the move! No box can contain Him!

Every evening as we sat around tables with our eyes glued to these huge multimedia screens and heard story after story of what God was doing around the world, we couldn't help but agree with the nightly theme at Cape Town 2010: "God is on the move!" And in ways we could never have predicted or even imagined. *Never!*

Whichever way you look at it today, God is on the move, big time! But come to think of it, God has always been on the move. Right from the beginning of beginnings: "In the beginning God created the heaven and the earth. The earth was formless and void, and darkness was over the surface of the deep, and the Spirit of God was moving over the surface of the waters."[44]

AS IN THE DAYS OF ACTS

God is on the move, so are people! Actually, people are on the move *because* God is on the move. I am absolutely convinced that people movements are God movements. He certainly moved my entire nuclear family from Ghana to Canada, using the same word He spoke to move Abraham from Haran to the land of Canaan.[45]

God moves people for a season or a lifetime but always for a reason: to get to spread His fame or to get them to know His name. So whether to hear the Gospel or to spread it, people are on the move like never before in our world today because God is on the move more than ever before in these dying minutes of time in the face of imminent eternity.

Recently I have really been enjoying reading through the Acts of the Apostles over and over again and been freshly amazed at the parallels for our world on the move today.

FOR WHATEVER SEASON; BUT ALWAYS FOR A REASON

Dr. Luke records in the seventeenth chapter of his second book to one Theophilus how Apostle Paul stood up and boldly addressed the people of Athens at the Aeropagus saying, "From one man he made every nation of men, that they should inhabit the whole earth; and he determined the times set for them and the exact places where they should live."[46]

It is God who determines the migratory movements we see in our world today. People think they are moving for greener pastures, to escape war, for political asylum, because their company transferred them, or to get a foreign degree or diploma, but the majority do not realize that ultimately it is God who moved them!

And you know why? "God did this so that men would seek him and perhaps reach out for him and find him..."[47] God is sovereignly, massively moving people, including bringing hundreds of thousands of international students to Canada, that they might find Him.

Then there are those also who God sends to places in the world not to get their attention toward salvation per se, but that they may proclaim the Gospel, spread His fame! How else were the disciples supposed to send the Gospel to all Judea, Samaria, and to the ends of the earth without moving? In fact, the most rapid spread of the Gospel in the early years after Christ went back into Heaven was because of persecution, especially around and after the martyrdom of Stephen.

Hitherto, though the command to spread the Gospel beyond Jerusalem had been very clear,[48] the disciples largely stayed in Jerusalem. The Lord in His wisdom and sovereignty allowed the persecution to break out so that in their scurry, these 'people on the move' might be the ones to spread the

Gospel. And indeed, "Those who had been scattered preached the word wherever they went."[49]

It is amazing how many people from Latin America, Asia, and Africa have come to establish the Church in the West today. From reaching Quebecois, other Canadians, Asians, and Africans in the diaspora through church and leadership development to ministering to other geopolitical nationals through ISMC, obviously God moved me to Canada to spread His fame. Even at ISMC, we recently had a beautiful illustration of how God moves people to spread His fame.

NIGERIAN NEWBIES

When I became president of ISMC in 2013 I learnt that for years our ministry to international students in Brandon, Manitoba (a two-hour drive from Winnipeg) had folded up. No one was reaching the three hundred international students in that small city, mainly at the University of Brandon.

Today the story is different because by the summer of 2014 plans were far advanced to have a new ministry going on there. Indeed as I write this, a new weekly ministry to these students has been birthed, supervised by Nora, our new and capable associate staff there. But do you know who actually got the ministry started, catalyzed it, and were the "boots on the ground"? Two international students from Nigeria, Rabeh and Roy, who got to Brandon and literally said, "It is not right that there is no ISMC here!"

The Lord moved those young men from Nigeria not so much to get to know His name in Canada, but to spread His fame abroad!

A WORLD ON THE MOVE

Even the United Nations recognizes these unprecedented numbers of people on the move: "More people than ever are living abroad. In 2013, 232 million people, or 3.2 per cent of the world's population, were international migrants, compared with 175 million in 2000 and 154 million in 1990."[50]

The numbers tell the story:

- There are over **232 million** migrants in the world today.[51]
- The North, or developed countries, is home to 136 million international migrants, compared to 96 million in the South, or developing countries.[52] There is significant movement from everywhere to everywhere, nonetheless!
- In 2013, *half* of all international migrants lived in 10 countries, with the United States hosting the largest number (45.8 million), followed by the Russian Federation (11 million); Germany (9.8 million); Saudi Arabia (9.1 million); United Arab Emirates (7.8 million); United Kingdom (7.8 million); France (7.4 million); Canada (7.3 million); Australia (6.5 million); and Spain (6.5 million).[53]
- Among these top ten countries, no one beats the United States in absolute migration numbers, but per capita the top four migrant countries will be United Arab Emirates, Saudi Arabia, Australia, and Canada.[54]
- The UN refugee agency (UNHCR) reported on World Refugee Day in 2014 that the number of refugees, asylum-seekers and internally displaced people worldwide has, *for the first time in the post-World War II era*, exceeded 50 million people.[55]
- 51.2 million people were forcibly displaced at the end of 2013, fully 6 million more than the 45.2 million reported in 2012.[56]

STUDENTS AND SCHOLARS ON WHEELS AND WINGS

Of special interest to me in this book is the international student population in particular. In some circles they are also known as "mobile students." This category of people on the move are generally described as those studying outside their country of citizenship.

- There have always been international students,[57] but never in the numbers we're seeing today.
- Over the past three decades, the number of post-secondary students enrolled outside their country of citizenship has risen dramatically, from 800,000 worldwide in 1975 to 4.5 million in 2012, a more than *fivefold increase*.[58]
- During 2000-12, the number of foreign tertiary students enrolled worldwide *more than doubled* (from 2.1 million to over 4.2 million), with an average annual growth rate of almost 7 percent.[59]
- It is projected that **7.2 million** students may be enrolled abroad by 2025.[60]
- More than one in two foreign students (more than 50 percent) in tertiary education are enrolled in Australia, Canada, France, Germany, the United Kingdom, or the United States.[61]
- In absolute terms, the United States hosts most of these students, with 16 percent of all foreign students, followed by the United Kingdom (13 percent), Germany (6 percent), France (6 percent), Australia (6 percent) and Canada (5 percent).[62]
- Students from Asia represent 53 percent of foreign students enrolled worldwide. The largest numbers of foreign students from that continent are from China, India, and Korea.[63]
- After Asia, the next largest region that international students hail from is Europe (23 percent), followed by Africa (12 percent), Latin America and the Caribbean (6 percent), North America (3 percent) and Oceania (1 percent).[64]
- In 2012, the number of foreign students enrolled in tertiary education in OECD[65] countries was, on average, three times the number of students from OECD countries studying abroad.[66]

- Some 82 percent of all foreign students are enrolled in G20 countries, while 75 percent of all foreign students are enrolled in OECD countries. These proportions have remained stable during the past decade.[67]
- Europe is the top destination for students at the tertiary level of education enrolled outside their country of origin, hosting 48 percent of these students, followed by North America, which hosts 21 percent of all international students, and Asia with 18 percent.[68]
- The number of international students in Oceania has almost tripled since 2000, though the region hosts less than 10 percent of all foreign students.[69]
- Other regions, such as Africa, Latin America, and the Caribbean, are also seeing growing numbers of international students, reflecting the internationalization of universities in an increasing number of countries.[70]

CANADIAN CONTRIBUTION

I find Canada's place in all this very intriguing. Canada's migration rate is one of the world's highest. Canada, apart from being among the top ten migrant countries in absolute numbers (7.3 million in 2013), is the fourth per capita.

- An average of 250,000 immigrants in Canada each year since 1991.
  - o That means 684 per day; 28/hour.[71]
- Over 100,000 international students admitted *each* year since 2012.
- A record 491,547 Temporary Foreign Workers (TWF) allowed to work in Canada in 2012 (five times higher than in 2002).
  - o The number consisted of 213,573 new TFWs in 2012 and 277,974 already here.[72]
- From 2009 to 2013, Canada gave refugee status to 122,518 people.
  - o That is an average of 24,514 people in each year—67 per day.[73]

Today, Toronto is the most international city in the world, and Vancouver is actually the second-largest Sikh city in the world.[74] It is said that "worship on any given Sunday in Toronto occurs in more than 130 languages."[75]

While Canada is the seventh most popular destination for international students in the world after the USA, UK, Germany, France, Australia,[76] and China, in per capita terms it is only second to Australia.

Consider, for example, that although the United States has approximately one million international students for a population of about three hundred million people, today Canada has a third of that (three hundred thousand) for a population which is merely a tenth (thirty-five million) of the United States'. Thus, in per capita terms, Canada has become even more important than the United States in international student intake and impact.

International students comprise approximately 8 percent of all tertiary enrolments in Canada (8 percent of undergraduate, 16 percent graduate, and 26 percent doctoral). This is double the OECD average of 4 percent but notably below Australia (18 percent) and the UK (17 percent). In the US, meanwhile, the proportion of international students matches the average for OECD states: 4 percent.[77]

WHY CANADA?

If the Lord had given me a choice of country to move to (which I was seriously averse to until 2006 but couldn't help it in 2008), I, quite frankly, wouldn't have chosen Canada. Also, I would certainly not have chosen "French Canada" (Quebec), for that matter. But God is so much wiser. His ways are not our ways, neither are His thoughts like ours. As far as the heavens are above the earth, so much higher are His thoughts and ways above ours.[78]

The major factors in international students' choice of Canada are: safety (80 percent of respondents indicated this to be an "essential" or "very important" factor in their choice), the quality of education (78 percent essential or very important), and Canada's tolerant, welcoming society (76 percent).[79]

Other important factors include the opportunities for full-time work in Canada following studies (67 percent essential or very important) and cost of studying in Canada compared to other countries (64 percent).[80]

In "selling" their institution, University of British Columbia, after giving their accolades–including Vancouver's umpteen tourist attractions and the annoyingly mild weather (yes, I live in the cold and I'm jealous!)– also states:

- Canada has an excellent health care system and social services
- Canada is a safe country and study destination
- Canada has a well-developed and stable economy
- Canadians are friendly people with an open and welcoming culture.[81]

In two chapters' time, we will more fully delve into Canada's stories and stats.

BOTTOM LINE

Why is there all this movement across the globe of over two hundred-and-thirty million people? There are a myriad reasons I can think of: better geopolitics between most nations; an interest in promoting academic, cultural, social, and political ties among countries; ease of travel and cheaper costs; internationalization of the labor markets for highly skilled labor; political unrests and wars; a flatter world (according to Thomas Friedman) a.k.a. globalization, and so forth. While these are symptoms and outward manifestations, the root cause, is this: people are moving like never before because *God is on the move* more than ever before! People movements are God movements.

Looking at this through missiological goggles, and using international student statistics as an example, around the time the pivotal first International Congress on World Evangelization was held in Lausanne, Switzerland, there were about 800,000 post-secondary international students worldwide. By the time the next was held in Manila, Philippines, in 1989, the number had jumped to around 1.2 million. By the third in Cape Town, South Africa, the number of international students had escalated, almost quadrupled, to 4.2 million! (See OECD diagram below[82])

Why, oh why? Because all around the world, *"God is on the move!"* and it just makes sense to follow suit!

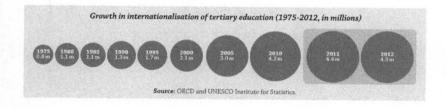

Growth in internationalisation of tertiary education (1975-2012, in millions)

| 1975 0.8 m | 1980 1.1 m | 1985 1.1 m | 1990 1.3 m | 1995 1.7 m | 2000 2.1 m | 2005 3.0 m | 2010 4.2 m | 2011 4.4 m | 2012 4.5 m |

Source: OECD and UNESCO Institute for Statistics.

~7~

IT JUST MAKES SENSE!

"Open your eyes and look"

"I will go anywhere, provided it be forward."
~DAVID LIVINGSTONE

They were dead serious about it. Even their Chamber of Commerce joined forces with the city to create an "It Just Makes Sense" campaign to persuade the WestJet airline company to make Fort St. John, nicknamed 'the Energetic City,' a destination for the Canadian airline.

The city of Fort St. John, located at Mile 47 along the Alaska Highway, is a city in north-eastern British Columbia, Canada, encompassing a total area of about 22 square kilometers (8.5 sq mi) with about 20,000 residents.[83]

Originally established in 1794 as a trading post, Fort St. John is said to be the oldest European-established settlement in present-day British Columbia. It is served by the Fort St. John Airport.[84]

WestJet did agree that, "As one of the northernmost populated centers in British Columbia, Fort St. John supports the surrounding rural area of over 69,000 people with a broad range of services and activities. The city's age is a stark contrast to its youthful demographic. Home to young couples and BC's highest birthrate, Fort St. John is full of community spirit and opportunity."[85] But were they going to put their money where their mouth was?

Residents wrote copious letters, as well as submitted lots of videos of friends, families, and work colleagues, dramatizing how "it just makes sense" to fly there. These were to be compiled and edited into a video as part of a thirty-minute presentation to WestJet executives in the city of Calgary. They yelled, they danced, they sang, "it just makes sense." Guess what? It worked.

After announcing their excitement about two new U.S. cities they were now flying to non-stop, WestJet added that, "We are also excited to announce the very first communities to be serviced by WestJet Encore; Fort St. John and Nanaimo in beautiful British Columbia." WestJet did announce that starting June 24, 2013, it would run daily flights from both Vancouver and Calgary to Fort St. John.[86]

Did it really just make sense for WestJet to start plying Fort St. John? For me, that is neither here nor there. That's their business decision. Let me tell you what *really* makes such theological and missiological sense to me that I'm prepared to yell, dance, sing...in a sustained national and international campaign to awaken, envision, engage, and resource the whole Church to optimize the most strategic Great Commission opportunities of our time!

COAST TO COAST CAMPAIGN

In my first year in office as ISMC president I flew the entire country of Canada—virtually every province *from sea to shining sea,* coast to coast. It was a strange feeling to savor both the Atlantic and Pacific in the space of a few days.

One of my high points was standing at Cape Spear (47.5236° N, 52.6194° W), right at the easternmost tip of the entire North American continent and trusting God to fill the whole continent with His glory.

I've interacted with thousands of believers, hundreds of leaders, preached in scores of churches, spoken on dozens of campuses, and you know what? The overwhelming majority of people 'get it'...but usually only *after* they have been exposed to the facts and figures about the inspiring, ongoing God stories of missions to and through international students.

Quite honestly, a few still don't get it, but for the majority who do, "it just makes sense!" after the Lord has mercifully opened their eyes to see!

"OPEN YOUR EYES AND LOOK"

> "My food," said Jesus, "is to do the will of him who sent me and to finish his work. "Don't you have a saying, 'It's still four months until harvest'? I tell you, **open your eyes and look** at the fields! They are ripe for harvest. Even now the one who reaps draws a wage and harvests a crop for eternal life, so that the sower and the reaper may be glad together. Thus the saying, 'One sows and another reaps' is true. I sent you to reap what you have not worked for. Others have done the hard work, and you have reaped the benefits of their labor."[87]
> (emphasis added)

Jesus had to tell His disciples to "open their eyes" (some versions say "awaken!"), because they were oblivious to how God was at work right among them! Right under their noses, not only was the life of a serially promiscuous woman radically changing forever, but a whole city was about to break out in revival. And yet they couldn't see. "I tell you, open your eyes and look," Jesus booms!

One of the most meaningful contemporary Christian songs I love says, "Open the eyes of my heart, LORD," by Paul Baloche. That, I have come to find, is a most pertinent prayer, for God can be seriously at work right under our noses and we may miss it. I think of Balaam the prophet whose donkey could see danger ahead and stopped; he didn't.[88] In fact, he beat the poor ass till the animal spoke and said something like, "And you call *me* stupid?!" Mercifully, "Then the LORD opened Balaam's eyes, and he saw the angel of the LORD standing in the road with his sword drawn. So he bowed low and fell face down."[89] But the Lord had to open his eyes!

I can never figure out how the eyes of Magi in the East were opened to an unusual star and followed it all the way to Jerusalem, a two-year expedition, to find the special child who had been born King, but no one in Jerusalem itself seemed to have taken a second look at the firmaments. Even worse were the scribes who, after hearing of this incredible narrative and were commissioned by the king to search the records, found Bethlehem as the specific location of this Savior of the world, but did not have the presence of mind to go themselves to see (if even not to pay homage)! Unbelievable!

How about those two disciples on the road to Emmaus who were telling Jesus about Himself and did not realize it was He! They even had the guts to tell Him, when He asked of the recent happenings in Jerusalem, about His own death, burial, and resurrection: "Are you the only one visiting Jerusalem who does not know the things that have happened there in these days?"

It was not until at table, after they had successfully persuaded Him to be a recipient of their hospitality, that when He took bread, gave thanks, broke it, and began to share it, "Then their eyes were opened and they recognized him, and he disappeared from their sight. They asked each other, "Were not our hearts burning within us while he talked with us on the road and opened the Scriptures to us?""[90]

Don't these few examples just make you wonder what we could be failing to see today, totally oblivious to, hidden in plain sight, so-to-speak? May the Lord mercifully open our eyes, too!

WHY WE SEE NOT

So back to Samaria. The disciples couldn't see. Could the things that blinded them be the very things blinding us today from seeing the bountiful harvest at our doorsteps, with the whole world so on the move today?

1. CONSUMERISM

In a way, I don't blame the poor dudes. These guys had been on the road for a long time; and they were just about halfway. They had left Judea en route northwards to Galilee. Samaria was on their way. They were tired, thirsty, and hungry. They had left Jesus in the town of Sychar, near the famous Jacob's well, to grab some "fast food" and would be back with some for Jesus, only to return to find Him chatting with a woman.

They were so consumed by their desire to satisfy their stomach stings, the last thing on their mind was souls and salvation. But He had a higher hunger that, when quenched, stilled the less important gastric hunger:

> *Meanwhile his disciples urged him, "Rabbi, eat something."*
>
> *But he said to them, "I have food to eat that you know nothing about." Then his disciples said to each other, "Could someone have brought him food?" "My food," said Jesus, "is to do the will of him who sent me and to finish his work."[91]*

Boy! And this was before Maslow's hierarchy of needs!

Is it not the same with many of us today? Many of us are not seeing the harvest of souls that is right here in our own backyard because of *consumerism*—the frenzy of getting the things we need and want for ourselves.

For the half a decade I've lived in North America so far, it hasn't ceased to amaze me how our minds are constantly playing to the tune of "Bills! Bills! Bills!" and the chorus of "Buy! Buy! Buy!"

And we grab stuff, even when we don't have the economic means, such that today the average Canadian owes $1.63 for every $1 dollar he earns.[92] How could we "open our eyes to see" anything else other than our belongings and bills!

2. CONCEPTION

The disciples had the "mindset" of a popular saying, *"It's still four months until harvest."* It probably was a number one Beatles-type hit, topping the pop charts in top cities like Jerusalem in those days. But Jesus was about to shift their paradigm by saying, "No, not four months till the harvest! Wake up guys! The harvest is here and now. It's in this woman and the many men who are just about to follow and come our way!"

Obstructed by their concept of mission, their missiology was not in sync with the Master's. They had a nice philosophical saying and mindset that had (mis)informed them that the harvest was "out there," both in terms of geography and timing. They were only *passing through* Samaria, remember? En route to God's people in Galilee. Who would ever think that anything significant would happen in Samaria—these folks tainted with Assyrian blood. Don't forget, Jews would not associate with skunky Samaritans.[93] Besides, it was lunch time and the sun was high up!

You mean right here in Samaria? Right now—at lunch time? And at this moment in history when *we* are *still* expecting a coming Kingdom? *"Come on, Jesus, this is one of those moments you make us wonder whether we made the right choice to follow you. Crazy!"*

People, as I travel the world, especially the major cities of North America, sometimes I find churches that are emptying, on the verge of closing down, crying for membership, and lonely foreigners passing right in front of their doors, crying for fellowship. And there's no connection!

It doesn't even register to many that the people they are looking for "out there" are "right here" and looking for them right now! And some of these churches, out of their meager budgets, still support missionaries trying to reach the Chinese in faraway Asia, but are totally blinded to the same Chinese the Lord Himself has brought across the Pacific, right to their doorsteps and backyards!

Perhaps even the disciples of Jesus' concept of mission may have been the gathering of *crowds* to hear Jesus preach and teach—not this lonely one-on-one conversation with a strange woman!

Many Christians still have a nineteenth/twentieth century concept of missions. When will we wake up and smell the coffee, get rid of our old paradigms and misconceptions like the disciples and realize that the harvest is not far away and sometime in the future, but right here and right now? The nations have come! Revival is imminent. We have never been closer to closing the Great Commission than in this generation!

3. CULTURE

Blinded by their culture (and traditions)—Jews wouldn't even associate with Samaritans, who they considered tainted Jews (oxymoron intended) because of Assyrian blood. And not just a Samaritan—a *woman* at that! Double trouble! And worse, *that kind* of woman?! Triple trouble! They were missing a huge harvest right under their noses. Are we also?

For fifteen years my Chinese church in Montreal had no pastor for the English congregation because they were searching for someone who looked like and talked just like them—Chinese! Boy, did God surprise them (and me!). And now that we might have to part (I've been 'interim' for three years; come on!), it is becoming a pretty tough transition for them and me. We have so grown to love each other.

The other day my wife was trying to get our troops (children) to hurry up to get to church for a special occasion. They knew we were going to a church (they can't even count the number and variety of churches they've been to in their short lives!) and wondered, "which one?" My wife inadvertently said, "The Chinese church." So when we finally pulled up to the building, my then four-year old daughter blurted out, "Oh! *Our* church." May she always be culture-blind, in a good way!

SAMARIA TODAY

"Samaria today" sounds like a really cool newspaper name. And when I begin to share with you shortly some of the things God is doing with international students in Canada, you'll see how what Jesus said in John 4 so much applies to our context today because we're reaping such an "easy harvest!"

We don't travel (God has brought these students to us using government and university strategies and desires); we don't pay to see them (their parents and governments pay huge sums of money to get them to come); we don't go door-to-door evangelizing or even try to learn their languages (they come to us—and want to learn English). Really, "others have done the hard work," like Jesus said, (including missionaries who have gone to these countries and suffered for the Gospel), and we are reaping the benefits of their labor!

But praise the Lord that He eventually opened the eyes of His disciples to see and experience a great harvest—or, well, it became rather too obvious, don't you think? Once we also get past these three blinding Cs—Consumerism, Conception and Culture—our eyes will be open to how "it just makes sense" to reach out and reap the harvest, here and now.

THEY ARE HERE!

The people we are looking for are right here among us, and looking for us...

Winnipeg is not the biggest city in Canada when it comes to migrants in general and international students in particular, but it surely is significant. Over six-thousand international students—not bad at all.

On one chilly November night (very typical of a city which has rightly been nicknamed "Winterpeg") I shared with the faithful from all sorts of denominations and local congregations who had gathered at Waverly Baptist Church to hear me speak on the huge missiological opportunity that lay before Canada with international students.

I shared how a growing number of Christian leaders, organizations and churches are becoming fed up with the Church spinning its wheels and now really want to *"count for zero"*[94]: zero languages without the Scriptures; zero people groups without disciple makers; zero people who have not heard the Gospel; zero villages or neighborhoods without a church.

Somehow, that night it was the Nepalese (whether from Nepal or Bhutan) that really were on my heart, since they are one of the least reached people groups in the world.

The point was made when we all saw from the LCD projection a Nepalese young lady named Itchya Karki, 19, in Kathmandu who was itching to come to Canada to study, specifically to the University of Guelph.[95] They are coming, and they are here. The people we are looking for to reach with the love of Christ and His good news are right here among us; and looking for us. And like in Samaria, both the potential harvest and the harvesters are right at our doors!

As I preached the next morning at Bethel Community Church, I got introduced to a Caucasian-Canadian couple who had just returned from Nepal. They revealed to me that there were six hundred Nepalese in the city and one of the Nepalese pastors they were helping is reaching at least 10 percent of them every Sunday. Reaching the unreached right within our reach.

Oh boy, and wasn't Jesus so right? Not only are the fields ripe and right here and right now, *"the saying 'One sows and another reaps' is true. I sent you to reap what you have not worked for. Others have done the hard work, and you have reaped the benefits of their labor.*[96] This huge movement of the nations to our backyards and doorsteps is nothing we envisaged, strategized, or paid for...I dare say, or even prayed for! For does He not do "exceeding abundantly above all that we ask or think?"[97]

It's amazing how hard governments and academic institutions are working to bring in these nations and how willing families are to sacrifice lots (money and more) just to send their children our way. All we do is wait, welcome, work, and watch God yield a harvest right before our eyes? Wow!

"It just makes sense." Forget Fort St. John. This one *really* does! Just "open your eyes and look!" Reaching these 4.5 million students on the move globally (and the three hundred thousand international students who have come to Canada in particular) is simply:

1. Statistically sensible
2. Scripturally sound
3. Stunningly simple
4. Strategically smart

Let me explain.

~8~

STATISTICALLY SENSIBLE!

Box or no box, the numbers make sense

"I believe that in each generation God has called enough men and women to evangelize all the yet unreached tribes of the earth. It is not God who does not call. It is man who will not respond!"
~ISOBEL KUHN

N umbers are important. True, *they ain't everything;* but surely they are important enough for God to place a whole "Book of Numbers" in the Pentateuch, the first five books of the Bible.

Looking at the numbers of internationally mobile students alone, it simply makes sense to reach out to the teeming population in Canada and elsewhere around the world.

CANADA COUNTS

Across all levels of study, there were 293,500 international students in Canada as at the end of 2013. This represents a five percent share of all of the world's internationally mobile students. The number of international students in Canada has increased by 84 percent over the last decade, and grew 22.8 percent from 2011 to 2012 alone and 11 percent from 2012 to 2013.[98]

As previously stated, Canada is among the top two international student destinations in the world per capita; and number seven in absolute numbers, after the US, the UK, France, Germany, Australia, and China.

At the end of the first decade of this new millennium there were barely 180,000 international students in Canada. A Ministry Effectiveness Project that ISMC commissioned in 2011 revealed that our mission was reaching less than two percent of those students at the time. Worse still, ISMC's ministry growth was not keeping pace with the rapid growth opportunity in international students.

In fact, up until the Lord called me to serve as ISMC president, the thirty-year old mission had done tremendous work out West, but no ministry anywhere east of Ottawa, Ontario (nil in Quebec and Atlantic Canada), an area representing at least 20 percent of the entire international student population in Canada—I labeled them "the forgotten fifth."

AGAIN I SAY, "GOD IS ON THE MOVE!"

Did the numbers wait for us to catch up? You bet not! In 2012 alone the government let 100,000 international students into the country. Historic! Record-breaking! In fact, to quote the February 26, 2013, government communique from Ottawa, "Canada welcomed a record number of international students in 2012, Citizenship, Immigration and Multiculturalism Minister Jason Kenney announced today. Last year was **the first time in Canadian**

history that Canada has welcomed over 100,000 international students, an increase of 60 percent from 2004."[99] (emphasis mine)

Again I say, "God is on the move!" To me, it is significant that anyone will say anything about something happening for the *first time* in a country that's a century-and-a-half years old! In nearly 150 years, only in this decade has Canada admitted over 100,000 international students in a single year. After the historic move in 2012 (104,829 admissions), the government repeated the feat in 2013 with 111,841 admitted into the country that year alone.[100] It seems to me there's no going back. This clearly tells me God is on the move! We had better open our eyes and look!

BUREAU BREWS

At their November 2014 annual conference, the forty-eighth of its kind, the Canadian Bureau for International Education (CBIE) released its annual global report on the state of international education in Canada[101] with the following highlights:

- In 2013 there were 293,505 international students in Canada, an 84 percent increase over the last decade and an 11 percent increase over the previous year
- 55 percent of international students intend to pursue additional studies in Canada following their current program
- 50 percent of international students intend to apply for permanent resident status in Canada in the future
- China remains the top sending country, with 32 percent of enrollments
- Nigeria and Russia head the list of fastest growing sending countries.[102]

E-V-E-R-Y-W-H-E-R-E!

They are here in their teeming numbers, and everywhere! Even some of the most "obscure" places in Canada have international students—and loads of them. Of course it goes without saying that tertiary institutions like University of Toronto, McGill, Université de Montréal, University of Alberta and University of British Columbia (UBC) each have more than seven thousand international students.

In fact, as of fall, 2013, the University of Toronto had over 12,600 international students on their three campuses from 150 countries![103] UBC has 10,181 from 149 countries.[104] One out of every four of their graduate students is an international.[105]

These institutions are not isolated cases, far from it. A recent survey revealed that "a significant majority of Canadian universities—82 percent— now place internationalization among their top five strategic priorities."[106]

These students come from "everywhere" and they are found "everywhere" in Canada. Most universities in Canada have become a mini United Nations, certainly a microcosm of a global village. The 300,000 international students in Canada hail from 194 countries.[107]

Are you beginning to see why it simply is a statistically sensible thing to reach out to these students? The numbers are compelling!

Source country	# of students (2013)	% of total IS population
China	95,160	32.42%
India	31,665	10.79%
South Korea	18,295	6.23%
Saudi Arabia	14,235	4.85%
France	13,090	4.46%
United States	12,065	4.11%
Japan	6,780	2.31%
Nigeria	6,080	2.07%
Mexico	5,370	1.83%
Iran	4,335	1.48%

Top ten source countries for international students in Canada, 2013. Source: CBIE[108]

DOUBLE DOWN, MAN!

International student enrollment grew from 136,000 in 2001 to over 265,000 in 2012—a **94 percent** increase! And guess what? As if we didn't have enough international students in Canada, the government wants to *double* the number of students by 2022!

The task force, spearheaded by the president of Western University, that worked on that report in 2012 wanted to see the number of international students shoot from 239,130 then to 450,000 in ten years—from kindergarten through Grade 12 and post-secondary institutions, without taking away seats from Canadians.[109]

Many institutions of learning, like University of Calgary, have already publicly stated they want to *double* their number of international students—and we know why, especially in the face of dire funding challenges for our tertiary institutions.[110]

It is interesting to note how journalists like Erin Millar argue that this "call to double foreign students signals a fundamental policy shift" in two main ways. "First, because post-secondary education is a provincial responsibility, the federal government typically avoids such discussions." So why is the federal government wading into this one?

"Second," she writes, "the fact that the report was presented to Ed Fast, Ministry of International Trade, rather than the Ministry of Human Resources and Social Development, illustrates how foreign students are now considered a key piece of Canada's global economic strategy, rather than an issue for universities to handle."[111]

It goes without saying that this is about economics more than anything else! In fact, the 122-page report was entitled *International Education, a Key Driver of Canada's Future Prosperity.*[112]

In that government communique I referred to earlier, Canada's Citizenship, Immigration and Multi-culturalism Minister Jason Kenney stated in no uncertain terms, "Attracting and retaining the best and brightest immigrants from around the world is part of the government's commitment to grow Canada's economy and ensure long-term prosperity."[113]

Of course, you wouldn't think the government of Canada loves international students *that much* for just who they are. This is about economics—that's the bottom line. International students contribute more than $8 billion every year to the Canadian economy.[114] Eight billion? Oh, yes!

And it's not just Canada. Globally, international education is a $2.2 trillion industry.[115] At least some officials are honest about the bottom line: "Overall, the total amount that international students spend in Canada is greater than our export of unwrought aluminum ($6 billion), and even greater than our export of helicopters, airplanes and spacecraft ($6.9 billion) to all other countries," consultant Roslyn Kunin states.[116]

Erin Millar then puts another interesting twist on these economic indicators: "If education is considered an export, its value is striking compared to traditional exports to particular countries. Education accounts for 44% of exports to Saudi Arabia, 28% to India and 19% to Korea."[117]

DOUBLE, YES; 2022, NO!

With this backdrop, it is no wonder that when the federal government came out with their desire to see a doubling of international students in Canada by 2022, the provincial governments of Ontario and British Columbia (the two top destinations for international students) were literally laughing at the long range idea. They want to double the number of international students much sooner!

Even back in 2010, two years before the federal government report to double, the province of Ontario had set a five-year goal to attract 50% more international students to its colleges and universities. Guess what? By the close of 2014, a full year ahead of schedule, they had *already surpassed* that by some nearly ten thousand students.[118]

Is it any wonder? In 2012, for example, international students were one of British Columbia's top five earners. In fact, international students raked in more money for BC ($1.8 billion) in 2010 than they got from crop and animal production.[119] In an article in the *Vancouver Sun* in which Martin Randall[120] basically wanted to make the point that education is a major contributor to GDP and that young foreign students can help address future job shortages in BC, he wrote:

> *International Education is among the top five export sectors in B.C., with significant contributions to the provincial economy. In 2010, international students spent over $1.8 billion on tuition, accommodation and discretionary spending. The provincial GDP generated was equivalent to $1.2 billion,*

slightly greater than that from the crop and animal production industry ($1.1 billion) and almost as large as that from the logging and forestry industry ($1.6 billion). An upcoming economic impact update commissioned by BCCIE suggests that these numbers have grown each year since.[121]

It is true that "in addition to making a significant contribution to our economy, international students bring new perspectives and cultures to our campuses, enriching the learning experience of all students,"[122] as Paul Davidson, President of the Association of Universities and Colleges of Canada, asserts, but really, if truth be told, the bottom line is the bottom line.

I HAVE A PROBLEM

OK, first, I *don't* have a problem. I don't have a problem with the governments and academic institutions wanting to increase the numbers to increase their profits. Why should I? For them, it is a statistically sensible thing to do. After all, governments must do what governments must do.

But I *do* have a problem. I've been crisscrossing the second widest country on earth (yes, Canada is, after Russia) screaming, "Guess who *else* should be doing the math?!" The Church! The Body of Christ! By the close of 2014, I was yet to find a single strategic document by a church or even denomination that recognized this huge missiological opportunity and had prescribed concrete, specific, measureable, attainable, time-bound measures to take full advantage of it. At the time of writing this, I'm still yet to stumble across one.

Yet, intentionally and strategically reaching these international students just makes so much sense—they are multitudinous—it is a statistically sensible thing to do! The three hundred thousand international students in Canada are not just numbers; *each* single one has a soul with an eternal destination.

Arise, Church, and do the math! After all, does your constitution and manifesto not compel you to?

~9~

SCRIPTURALLY SOUND!

Thinking inside the book

"The Bible is not the basis of missions;
missions is the basis of the Bible."
~RALPH WINTER

Spot on, Ralph Winter, spot on. Indeed as Nina Gunter also put it, *"If you take missions out of the Bible, you won't have anything left but the covers."* If you are a "person of the Book,'" if you are even remotely versed in the Holy Scriptures, I don't need to convince you that it is a Scripturally sound thing to reach out to these teeming international students with love and holistic care—and in very practical ways, for that matter.

The coolest thing (did I say "coolest"? There are so many cool things about this God phenomenon, I must have said something else is the "coolest" already!) about this international student spectacle is that while Jesus gave us a command to "Go into all the world and preach the good news,"[123] what has become nicknamed "the Great Commission," today the world has rather *come* to us! How cool is that?

So whether we go into the world or stay and receive the world that comes to us, it is a Scripturally sound thing to "preach the good news to all the world." Like the motto of the Christian primary school I had the privilege of attending in Accra, Ridge Church School, reminds me very often, "Not only with our lips, but in our lives."

BIBLE 101

We have already established, from Acts 8:4 and Acts 17:26–27, that people movements are God movements and that God is sovereignly bringing students to Canada to spread His fame, or that they might get to know His name (find Him). When I think of this, I'm also reminded of how God intentionally chose the season of Pentecost, when He knew all the world would gather in Jerusalem, to pour forth His Holy Spirit. The Holy Spirit would speak through the 120 faithful gathered in the upper room in different languages so that people from all the nations who had come, even from as far as Libya, would hear the Gospel in their mother tongue.

That day, the same God who once scattered the nations at Babel in the Old Testament using a variety of languages, gathered them again in the New Testament through a variety of languages.

At that time there were devout Jews from every nation living in Jerusalem. When they heard the loud noise, everyone came running, and they were bewildered to hear their own languages being spoken by the believers.

They were completely amazed. "How can this be?" they exclaimed. "These people are all from Galilee, and yet we hear them speaking in our own native languages! Here we

are—Parthians, Medes, Elamites, people from Mesopotamia,
Judea, Cappadocia, Pontus, the province of Asia, Phrygia,
Pamphylia, Egypt, and the areas of Libya around Cyrene,
visitors from Rome (both Jews and converts to Judaism),
Cretans, and Arabs. And we all hear these people speaking
in our own languages about the wonderful things God has
done![124]

Well, He's doing it again. He's bringing literally "every nation" into one crucible, this time in major cities in Canada, the USA, and the like, where they can hear the Gospel unhindered and critically explore it without fear. And this time language is not an issue—they all are students of Canada's lingua franca, English and/or French.

The first time many of these students ever get to see or hold a Bible is when they come to Canada. How can I ever forget the fire in her eyes and the passion with which this petite Chinese student, who was visiting the Winnipeg FOCUS (Friendship for Overseas College and University Students) Club of ISMC, yearningly said to me, "I want to study [the] Bible!"

JESUS THE STRANGER

True, Jesus and His parents were once internationals in Egypt—refugees fleeing persecution in their home country of Israel. But that was a couple of millennia ago.

If I came to church *today,* raised my hand during "testimony time" and said I had Jesus over at my house on the weekend, many would wonder what I'd been smoking. The counselors would wonder whether I'm on illegal drugs or gone off my prescribed ones!

But hey! Whenever we welcome an international student, "a stranger," we welcome Jesus Himself.

It's been awesome picking Jesus up at the airport and fetching Him some furniture to settle down. He loves it when my staff and I get Him into a warm, loving Christian home and feed and house Him, especially when the university kicks its students out during breaks.

Did you know Jesus loves Canadian stuff like apple picking, and has a blast during our Friday Focus club nights? He really appreciates it when we help Him with English as an Additional Language (EAL)—I guess it's quite different from Hebrew and Aramaic, especially navigating all the weird North American colloquial expressions like, "Can I pick your brain?" What?!

Those who don't know it's Jesus will be surprised when all is said and done:

> *When the Son of Man comes in his glory, and all the angels with him, then he will sit on his glorious throne. Before him will be gathered all the nations, and he will separate people one from another as a shepherd separates the sheep from the goats. And he will place the sheep on his right, but the goats on the left. Then the King will say to those on his right, 'Come, you who are blessed by my Father, inherit the kingdom prepared for you from the foundation of the world. For I was hungry and you gave me food, I was thirsty and you gave me drink, I was a stranger and you welcomed me... Then the righteous will answer him, saying, 'Lord, when did we see you hungry and feed you, or thirsty and give you drink? And when did we see you a stranger and welcome you...?' And the King will answer them, 'Truly, I say to you, **as you did it to one of the least of these my brothers, you did it to me.'**[125] (emphasis added)*

And for those, and there are many, who did not care it was Jesus...well... do well to finish that chapter!

THIS ONE I DON'T HEAR MUCH

It will be strange to come across a Christian who doesn't know the royal law in the Scriptures, "Love your neighbor as yourself."[126] What is surprising is how many don't know that the same Scriptures, in fact that same book and chapter (Leviticus 19), only sixteen verses later also says, "Love the *stranger* as yourself!"[127] (emphasis mine)

This is plain old hospitality. Some, in so-doing have entertained angels unknowingly;[128] others have welcomed future presidents, church leaders, and other significant future leaders without knowing. If you knew for sure that some international student needing a place to spend a couple of nights before the semester begins was going to become the next president of a wealthy oil state, would your attitude towards him change—even *slightly?*

Do not neglect to show hospitality to strangers, for thereby some have entertained angels unawares.[129] If the hoteliers and innkeepers in Joseph and Mary's day had known that this young unassuming couple was carrying the hope of the world, the desire of nations, the Son of God, they probably would've done more than offer a barn as a last resort.

I maintain that if there ever was a country that should know how to welcome and love strangers, it's Canada! Because really, unless you are of First Nations ("native Indian") descent, you came from somewhere. Even if it was four hundred years ago. You know the primary reason God gives as a basis for this command to "love the stranger as yourself?" He says, *for you were once foreigners yourselves!*[130]

God's ideal is that we treat the foreigner as properly as we would treat a citizen. And if you are a true Christian, this should be your aim, irrespective of your color or political persuasion. *"The foreigner residing among you must be treated as your native-born. Love them as yourself, for you were foreigners in Egypt. I am the LORD your God.*"[131] It is bad not to treat the foreigner like a bona fide citizen, and worse not to be hospitable at all. But to stoop as low as taking advantage of him or mistreating him...Scripturally, that is way below the belt: *"Do not take advantage of foreigners who live among you in your land."*[132] *"When a foreigner resides among you in your land, do not mistreat them."*[133]

"INTERNATIONAL STUDENTS OR 'CASH COWS'?" WHO CARES?

You may recall that I intimated earlier that in 2010 the province of Ontario set a five-year goal to attract 50 percent more international students. *The (Toronto) Star* reported in 2014 how *"a year ahead of schedule, Ontario has topped its goal of attracting 50 per cent more to its colleges and universities."*[134] The aim in 2010 was to boost the numbers to 57,000 (not counting kindergarten to high school). As at *Christmas 2014* they were already at 66,417 (43,159 in university and 23,258 at community college).[135]

"Why these goals?" one may ask? It's called *economics.* "We've met the goal ahead of schedule, but my thinking is we need to go beyond that—especially with graduate students," said Reza Moridi, Ontario's minister of training, colleges, and universities in an interview (he himself once an Iranian international student). "Each international student contributes about $35,000 to our economy, and $35,000 is creating a job, right?" he added.[136]

The (Toronto) Star article cited above was actually entitled, *"International Students or 'Cash Cows'?"* and posed a poignant question in its subtitle: *"These global whiz kids pay three or four times more tuition than their Ontario peers, but are they getting the cultural support and health services they need?"*

Some academic institutions do a super job of watching out for these students and seeing to their overall needs and well-being beyond the classroom (almost leaving my ISMC staff and me unemployed, except for taking care of the spiritual dimension of their lives). But by-and-large this is too much work for many academic institutions. It will take the community, especially the Christian community, "the people of the Book" which says, *"Do not take advantage of foreigners who live among you in your land,"* to *"love the stranger"* as we ought. Nobody else can like we can; nobody else will like we will.

From summer 2013 to summer 2014, ISMC, for example, made over 20,000 connections with international students blessing them with friendship, families, fun, food, forums, forays, and fellowship. Love the foreigner! Why? The Bible says so. Period.

CHRISTMAS COWS

The conversation with Josselin (pronounced *en Francais*) started with great excitement, but left me in deep sobriety. Of course I am glad whenever I encounter an international student, but I was ecstatic this time for many reasons.

Though I'm from Africa myself, I don't recall ever meeting anyone from Nouakchott, Mauritania, which is further north with 90 percent of its land in the Sahara Desert. Its full official name is *"Islamic Republic of Mauritania"* and though a former French colony, the official language is Arabic.

Are you beginning to appreciate why I was so excited? And this was a young woman at that, from a country which is well-known for atrocious human rights abuses like female genital mutilation and modern-day slavery. It was only in 1981 that Mauritania became the last country in the world to *sort of* abolish slavery. Today it is estimated by *SOS Slavery* that up to six hundred thousand people (20 percent of the population) are still enslaved.[137] *Global Slavery Index* estimates that as rather 160,000 (4 percent of the population) and ranks Mauritania as having the highest proportion of people in slavery of any country in the world![138]

Can you imagine that by now I was shaking in sheer excitement that Josselin had come from such a background to begin medical school at Université de

Montréal?! She's not on scholarship and her father is not in government (actually her father was exiled for a long time for speaking out against slavery).

I cared enough to give her a ride to campus, because that is what Christians do. We care. So here she was in the front seat of our family van, driving along and chatting. My jaws dropped (and thank God I did not leave the steering wheel) when she told me how much she was paying per semester for her program! My mind immediately went to that recent article in *The (Toronto) Star* cited above entitled, *"International Students or 'Cash Cows'?"*

Does anybody really care about these international students apart from what we get from them? When we *"were separate from Christ, excluded from citizenship in Israel and foreigners to the covenants of the promise, without hope and without God in the world,"*[139] God so loved us that He gave us His only begotten Son at Christmas. And Christmas was approaching.

In many cultures, like mine, it is humans who make sacrifices to deities. God turned this on the head when, instead of demanding a sacrificial cow from us for our myriad transgressions, He rather gave us His own Son as a sacrifice.

During Christmas 2013, my family and I were away to celebrate the first Christmas in six years with our parents and siblings! But I'm mighty glad that for Christmas 2014, we had twenty-three people from eleven countries under our roof, a third of them international students (like Josselin) from Brazil, France, Ghana, Tanzania, India, Nigeria, and the Philippines.

In a Christmas letter, I challenged the ISMC community of staff and donors alike: "This Christmas, will you too reach out to a hitherto Canadian 'Cash Cow' (international student) and mirror the love of the Father by rather sacrificing for them (offering a Christmas homestay or meal, giving to ISMC to reach them, etc.)? By this, people like Josselin will believe!"

TRAGEDY OF TRAGEDIES

In a recent twenty-one-day prayer and fasting period, I felt led to specifically ask those who had met to pray, to stand on 2 Chronicles 7:14 to beg God to forgive our land, Canada.

Upon our many sins as a nation, we had heaped sin upon sin by not just mistreating an international student, but killing one. And beyond that, dishonoring and dismembering the body.

In 2012, by the Lord's own doing, I found myself smack in the middle of praying, planning, and putting on a mourning and prayer service for the city of Montreal in response to the gruesome murder of a Chinese international student, Jun Lin. This was in my role as interim pastor of MCAGC; I was not even serving with ISMC then (speak of "connecting the dots").

You will find the story all over the internet about this young man, a Chinese national and Canadian resident studying at Concordia University in Montreal, who suddenly disappeared in late May, 2012.[140] Lin was last seen alive entering Luka Magnotta's Montreal apartment on May 24, 2012. A day later, a video surfaced online that showed Magnotta stabbing and dismembering Lin's lifeless body. It was titled "One Lunatic, One Ice Pick."[141]

Jun Lin's torso was found shortly after in a Montreal trash pile, while other body parts were shipped to the offices of Canadian federal political parties and Vancouver schools.[142] Magnota even parcelled and mailed the foot to the Prime Minister's office.[143] Abominable!

Lin's head remained missing until one Sunday, over a month later, when authorities confirmed that a severed human head found near a small lake in Angrignon Park, a vast green space in Montreal's south western region, belonged to the murdered Chinese student.

Jun had been gruesomely murdered by a Caucasian-Canadian "friend." Luka Magnotta was eventually arrested in Europe where he had fled. Magnotta was extradited from Berlin, Germany, after an international manhunt tracked him down in an internet café, where he was reading online news reports about himself.[144]

At the said mourning and prayer service, a joint collaboration by various Chinese churches, I was privileged to be one of two pastors (the other Chinese) to lead the congregation in intercessory congregational prayer for the city. Oh, boy did I cry out to the Lord!

JUSTICE...SORT OF

Although the trial did not start until 2014, when it did, Canada tried to "right the wrong'" (could we ever, really?). Finally in December 2014, the murderer was found guilty: "Luka Rocco Magnotta has been found guilty," the news read, "on all counts in the murder and dismemberment of Chinese engineering student Jun Lin, in a trial that hinged on Magnotta's mental state at the time of the grisly killing. It took the eight women and four men on the jury eight days of deliberation to reach a verdict."

"The jury also found Magnotta guilty of criminally harassing Prime Minister Stephen Harper and other MPs, guilty of mailing obscene and indecent material, guilty of committing an indignity to a body, and guilty of publishing obscene materials."[145]

Even in this dastardly devilish act, God supremely worked. The best part of all of this is that the late Jun Lin's mother (you wouldn't have been able to bear the sights and sounds of her excruciating wailing at the said service), as a result of this torturous experience (and this was her only son!!) has come to accept Jesus as her personal Lord and Saviour!! Hallelujah!

This is yet another victory for Christ in the midst of evil. Just like Joseph said to his brothers, *"Even though you planned evil against me, God planned good to come out of it."*[146]

My senior pastor at MCAGC was prompted to seek out this heart-wrenched woman when she landed in Montreal from China and shared the Gospel of Jesus Christ with her. She accepted the Lord and was baptised at our church the weekend before the prayer service we conducted—actually sharing her testimony was the major motivation for us holding that service as a means of evangelism, and did the media take the bait! [Although they tried very hard to avoid reporting her conversion portion of the story. The best part. Ah!]

This was a high profile case; the media was all over. I granted interviews to CTV, CBC Television, and CBC Radio. We had people contacting us when they saw me on TV to encourage us in our quest to do our little to impact our 'Jerusalem.'

You know the thing about retributive justice, right? It may throw "the beast" in jail but doesn't quite do much for the victim. I can understand why Dira Lin, father of the late Jun, would say that while "he is satisfied justice has been served, he is disappointed Magnotta never took the stand to explain his actions."[147] "The father came here for a few things," Urbas, his lawyer, said. "He wanted to honor his son, he wanted to find out why, he wanted to see justice done and he would like to hear some apology from the accused, now the convicted."[148]

IMAGINE IT WAS YOUR SON

Jun Lin's mother has been sick and remained in China while his father was in Montreal for much of 2014, attending the trial. He, too, was faithfully coming to our church (here in Montreal) literally every Sunday as long as he was in town. He was even at a Chinese-Quebecois wedding I was officiating early in the new year (2014), at another church.

It hasn't been easy for Dira Lin. He has a long way to go in his discipleship. It was reported that "a week after his son Jun's killer was sentenced to life in prison, Dira Lin said there would be no forgiveness for Luka Magnotta." "I think it will be better after time passes," he said. "I will keep thinking, my son, Magnotta, why did it happen?"[149] He couldn't sleep very well throughout the trial; he felt tired, his hair turned white. His present has been hijacked; his future is in limbo—imagine being out of home and out of work for a year!

When ISMC advertises "Friends for Dinner," a hospitality program we run in conjunction with churches in various cities across Canada to have their families host an international student for Thanksgiving, Easter, or Christmas, the standard poster begins with these words: "IMAGINE YOUR SON OR DAUGHTER SPENDING CHRISTMAS ALONE IN A FAR AWAY COUNTRY…"

As one who pastors the church Dira Lin attends when he is in Montreal, as well as serves as president of ISMC, what really cut me to the heart was when Dira "spoke of a loss his family will never get over, and of a **son who came to him, telling him that he wished to study in a city his father had never heard of: Montreal.**"[150] (emphasis mine) Now can you imagine that son or daughter, your *only one*, never spending Christmas again in your own country or any other even far away because *he is dead?*!

The other Sunday as my family was having lunch at the church (we usually have a fellowship meal every Sunday), I couldn't help but notice Dira Lin hanging around us, so drawn to our children. He eventually braved it and picked up our daughter, intrigued by her braids, and asked people around to take a photo of them (see picture). I couldn't help but get deeply saddened, yet even I could only imagine, "He must sorely miss his son, his only son."

Dira Lin and our daughter Nana Ashede

GAME CHANGERS

If we Christians don't rise up and take our mandate of hospitality seriously, the fate of the brimful number of internationals flooding our countries is dire, and the hope of the Gospel, dim.

But all is not dark and gloom; that is why mission agencies like ISMC exist. While some people harm students and their families (whether financial, physically, or emotionally) and make parents regret ever saying "yes" to their wards going to a faraway land to study, others, like "Papa John," make families think the best thing that ever happened in their lives was sending their son/daughter to Canada!

In his January 2015 newsletter, John Cudderford (my University of British Columbia campus director in Vancouver, who has been biologist, pastor, and now missionary with us) made *me* smile:

The students refer to me in various ways. Some simply call me "John." Others call me "Pastor John," "Uncle John" or even "Papa John." Now while I have to admit the latter appellation makes me smile, these last two speak to a reality that happens as I walk beside these students; I become part of their family. The family God gives them as they leave their biological family behind. The one that Snow, who came to faith through SFU Focus Club and now serves God full-time on campus, refers to as God's "Big Family."[151]

He continues:

In this "Big Family" of God's, it's always an honour to meet the biological family of the students we've come to know and love. This usually happens at convocation, such as M.'s this past spring. To finally meet the parents who've come to faith through her was wonderful. But **to hear them express their gratitude to me for looking out for and helping their daughter**—that was truly humbling. They, like other parents I've met, trust me as an "uncle."

Dr. John Cudderford concludes beautifully thus:

Being an "uncle" to some of these students not only means a wonderful connection with their parents here in Canada when we finally meet. It has also meant heartfelt invitations to connect with them once again in China. I have received many such invitations and plan to meet with some of these parents when I'm visiting students in the cities in which they live. Especially for those parents who are not yet Christians, perhaps meeting someone of a similar age and stage (Jooling and I know what it's like to have children studying overseas) will be used by God for His purposes in their lives. I am prayerfully planning who to meet, where and when.

John did make that trip to China in the summer of 2015 and has a bookfull of heartening stories to share.

Throughout history, hospitality has been a great door-opener to remarkable destinies. I think of Abraham and the three men and Rahab, the prostitute who hosted the two Israelite spies.

The change of location brings people into contact with information they otherwise may have never encountered. But it also finds them at a most vulnerable time—when their usual protections of family, friends, and culture are not around. And for some, it's rather that their danger has now been removed; for many, it is the first time they may find themselves in an environment where they are free to explore truth without fear of judgment, arrest, or death.

Even in the history of missions in Ghana, it is noted that as far back as 1835 two Asante princes, international students on their way to England, were brought to faith by the first English Methodist missionary before his early death.[152]

"THE GOD OF THE CANADIANS"

Bruce and Kirsten Littlejohn are serious about this Leviticus command to "welcome the stranger," "love the stranger as yourself." This lovely elderly couple (both in their seventies) who have deep missionary roots going back to the late sixties and seventies in Belgium, India, and Nepal with George

Verwer's OM (Operation Mobilization) are still going strong. They also spent fifteen years with SIM in Bangladesh.

Recently I went to preach at their church in Cochrane, near Calgary (Alberta), where their pastor decided to honor them for their faithful service to international students through ISMC since they came back to Canada in 1992. In both morning services, there was a rousing, spontaneous applause and standing ovation. Greater will be their heavenly crowd and crown.

During my interactions after my presidential inauguration in Edmonton on 12th July, 2013, I heard a story involving the Littlejohns that gave me goosebumps.

It particularly hit home because I had just come back from a Lausanne leaders' consultation in Bangalore, India. Bright-eyed Sangeeta Guha shared with my wife and me how she arrived at the Calgary International Airport and was stranded. She had come as an international student from India to pursue a Master's degree and had neither booked a means of transportation from the airport nor a place to stay. You may say, "third world thinking," "pretty bad planning" or whatever. Maybe. But God had a plan.

Bruce happened to be at the airport that fateful day. You see, that is one of the things Bruce and Kirsten do—pick international students up from the airport as a form of ministry. You will never forget the first person who picked you up from the airport, will you? The other thing Bruce is noted for nationwide is picking up unwanted furniture and fixing them up to become good enough for the Queen! He delivers these to strangers (international students) in need of them and this becomes such a door-opener to friendship and sharing of the Gospel in unimaginable ways!

I recently saw Kirsten with a hijab-clad electrical engineering PhD student from Iran, E., who had really taken to her because of contact through this type of ministry. The lady even came to hear me share my testimony and preach the Gospel the last time I spoke at the University of Calgary. She also lived with the Littlejohns for two years. Why would M., another Muslim PhD student (engineering) from Teheran bother to visit the Littlejohns and go through a six-week DVD series (*Stranger on the Road to Emmaus*) with them, but in response to the love they had shown her in welcoming the stranger and furnishing her room?

Bruce and Kirsten emailed me a photograph with M. at her recent graduation. The year before, when her parents visited from Teheran, she so much wanted them to meet the Littlejohns, so they invited these Iranian parents for lunch. Then they learnt that her father had been an international student in the United States in the sixties himself (also engineering and now government employed).

He shared how he had had contact with Christians then and that had been a positive part of his time in the West. "God works in wonderful ways is all we can say to that," Bruce and Kirsten assert. He very happily accepted a book entitled *By this NAME* as long as Bruce signed it. The book is very much the same as the DVD series. The Littlejohns, rather than *keeping their fingers crossed,* know too well that it is much more productive to *keep their knees bent* in prayer that God will work His purposes out in this Iranian family.

So, back to Sangeeta. She not only got a ride, but since she had no definitive destination per se, Bruce and Kirsten hosted her in their home. I bet there's no way you will be able to guess how long their guest stayed! No, not three days; three weeks may still surprise you, but no. Three months? No, three *years*!

Not many will do this, but you see, when we take God's Word seriously, we reap the serious results we read about in Scripture and marvel.

Do you know what this deep show of love to a stranger did to Sangeeta? Here she was, so well-taken care of by people who did not know her from Adam (or Eve), who did not look like her or talk like her. Her heart was so deeply touched, she said to my wife and me, "After a while, I began to search for the god of the Canadians." Wow!

And you know the nature of our God: "If you look for me whole-heartedly, you will find me."[153] Needless to say, Sangeeta is a strong believer in and follower of Jesus Christ today. She currently works for the Canadian government and is based in Edmonton. She even significantly contributes to the work of the Lord in diverse ways. For instance at our thirtieth anniversary banquet in Calgary, she donated very beautiful paintings to be presented as awards to deserving members of the ISMC fraternity!

I usually tease her that she thought she was coming to Canada to get a Master's; but really ended up with *the* Master! (She actually has three Master's degrees and a PhD now).

Is anyone also searching for "the god of the Americans" or the "god of the South Africans" or "god of the Australians" or simply put, *your* God because they've been so profoundly touched by the warmth of your welcome and the love you showed them, a hitherto stranger?

Folks! No one can love strangers like we Christians can (i.e. the truly Scripturally sound ones). If we're not, no one is! And it's pretty simple to.

*My wife and I with Sangeeta at my presidential inauguration
in Edmonton, July 12, 2013.*

~10~

STUNNINGLY SIMPLE!

The mission has never been easier

*"Our God of Grace often gives us a second chance,
but there is no second chance to harvest a ripe crop."*
~KURT VON SCHLEICHER

On a recent mission trip to Ghana I traveled with my short-term team to Cape Coast, a two-hour drive from the capital, Accra. It lies on a low promontory jutting into the Gulf of Guinea of the Atlantic Ocean about seventy-five miles (one hundred and twenty kilometers) southwest of the Ghanaian capital. Cape Coast was actually the first colonial capital of Gold Coast, as Ghana was known back then.

Today, Cape Coast is most famous for its castle constructed by the Swedes in 1653, originally built for trade in timber and gold but later used in the trans-Atlantic slave trade to hold humans. On his July, 2009 trip to Ghana, the United States president, Barak Obama, and his family made sure they stopped by this famous castle. It is arguably the most prominent of thirty such large commercial forts ("slave castles") dotted along Ghana's coastline.

TOUGH CALL

But what a lot of tourists (and even locals) do not know—or maybe even do not care—is that right within its environs, literally in its shadow, barely two hundred meters away, stands another monument of gargantuan historic proportions; with significant eternal ramifications.

The mission team and I had just come back from a thorough tour of Elmina Castle, so we decided that rather than do a similar tour at Cape Coast, we would visit this monument of which I speak so highly: the Wesley Chapel (1838). That was no tough call at all!

On the outside it seems like just another "plain old church," which happens to have the statue of the first Methodist missionary to Ghana in the front courtyard, facing the Cape Coast Castle. This was the maiden chapel at Cape Coast.

For me, the real treasure in Wesley Chapel is found underneath the pulpit. Buried under the pulpit are a man and two couples, the earliest European Methodist missionaries who came to the Gold Coast and died. Don't forget that at this time the west coast of Africa had been picturesquely named "the white man's graveyard," mostly because of malaria.

This sentence from William Fox's writings of 1851 gripped me: "The year 1837—one of unprecedented Mortality—Eight Deaths in nine Months."[154] For me, that account spanning from the Sierra Leone coast to the Gold Coast of West Africa, summarizes the history of modern missions in that region over the past two hundred years.

Let me just use the brief history of these first European Methodist missionaries in the Gold Coast as a vivid summary of the generally morbid missionary missive: James Dunwell—first missionary—arrived January 1,

1835, after an eleven-week journey. He died within six months at the young age of twenty-seven.

Fifteen months later, Rev. George and Harriet Wrigley (who were to replace Dunwell) arrived September 15, 1836. Rev. Peter and Mrs. Harrop (whose coming to work alongside the Wrigleys was a huge encouragement) arrived on January 15, 1837. Mrs. Harrop died just three weeks after her arrival. Her husband died three days later on February 8, 1837.

In fact, the very day thirty-year old Peter Harrop kicked the bucket, Harriet Wrigley also passed away (this was five months after landing on the shores of the Gold Coast). Nine months later, her husband George died too (fourteen months after arriving in Gold Coast).[155]

So these five lay buried underneath the pulpit of Wesley Chapel; and there are so many more of such stories, not just in Africa, but literally everywhere the Gospel has gone. More than enough has been written and said about the likes of Adoniram Judson and William Carey.

These forebears went at whatever cost, and today many of our brothers and sisters still do. Their attitude is summed up in the words of Thomas Birch Freeman "the father of Ghana Methodism," "It is necessary for me to go; but it may not be necessary to live."

In my opinion, when you compare that era of missions to now, to the nature of "home missions," reaching the world's internationals who gravitate toward our countries, the mission has never been easier. Let me tell you why:

1. Jesus said go—well, guess what? The nations have come!

The mandate in Matthew 28 to "go and make disciples of all nations" is very clear. For centuries this has meant physically going overseas on ships and planes. Yet today, go to any of our university campuses and you'll find people of almost every geopolitical state. Some universities boast of having over 160 different nationalities represented on their campuses.

Ever heard of the children's cartoons called *Veggietales*? Some of the episodes are hilarious. One of them features a group of people who unashamedly call themselves "Pirates who don't do anything." You know what I've labeled my ISMC staff? "Missionaries who don't go anywhere!" We "go and make disciples of all nations" yet we really don't go anywhere beyond our front steps and back yards!

Don't get me wrong. I'm not in any way belittling going to faraway places with the Gospel. That is still absolutely needed. The majority of those will never make it to our doorsteps in North America, Europe, or Australasia; but hey, do we not have a responsibility to steward the harvest right under our noses?

No travel and you are a missionary? Like seriously? The mission has never been easier!

2. **Logistically, no passport, no visa, no inoculations needed, no ships or planes**...the mission has never been easier.

I remember how I was shocked to the core upon hearing that in this day and age, a Nigerian compatriot of mine was almost denied a visa to India to attend a Lausanne meeting we were scheduled to be at in Bangalore just because he is a missionary. Eventually he was granted the visa on condition that he would not preach to anyone for the entire period he was going to be in India!

Those of us who hail from the Global South have loads of visa stories to tell. It is the general disposition of Western embassies that everyone who applies for a visa to Europe, North America, or "down under" wants to run away from their suffering and permanently settle in the West. That may be true of some, yes, but certainly not all. Time and space won't allow me to reveal many of the horrific stories.

But irrespective of whether one is from the east or west, when it comes to entering particular countries which perceive Christians (or Christianity) as a threat, none of us is immune.

Although I was quite exhausted after over 24 hours of traveling from Montreal through Detroit and Tokyo to Manila, my mind and spirit were agitated enough to sit up, get on my computer and send an email to my partners. Right about that time, 9:30 a.m. local time, I should've been en route to

Beijing, China, but I was not. Instead, I was sitting in a hotel in Manila and lamenting $418 of donor monies invested in this mission that had literally gone to waste because the ticket money could not be refunded. The reality of how much 'damage' what we do is to the core of the devil's operations hit me more than ever.

Barely a week before, I had received last minute news that the Chinese consulate in Ottawa had said they couldn't get me my visa before departing Montreal on March 17, 2014 (after them having possession of my passport and documents since February 25th). Not to mention the umpteen goings back-and-forth to get this document and that paper and what-not prior to that.

To be fair to them, instead of the three to five business days it usually takes to process a tourist visa, they had stated my pick-up time on my slip as "TBD" (to be determined), alerting me that working for an "NGO," my application would take longer than usual to scrutinize and process. Now it had been almost three weeks and because I had to leave for other engagements in Manila and needed my passport to travel, I had no choice but to withdraw my application only a couple of days prior to departure. So I did; and that meant the Beijing and Shanghai trips wouldn't materialize.

Upon hearing this, the following was a Canadian friend in Shanghai's response to this whole drama:

"Here is the translation of what happened:

- you are a pastor and the Chinese never had the intention of giving you a visa in the first place...period!
- but you are in a free country and you could take this incident to the media if they refused you your passport on the basis that you are a pastor
- so gently, ever so politely, they put you on notice that because you work for an NGO, because...because... because...and could you please come back...and come back again...

133

- in the end, they appear to want to give you a visa but you are the one who has given them too little time
- then you withdraw your application and maybe even apologize for your lack of understanding that they needed more time
- bottom line, they shift the blame on you when they did not have any intention of giving you a visa in the first place.

TIC .... This Is China.... Blessings on your trip to countries where they do what they say they do."

On that morning I speak of, just before firing the email to my President's Circle (those who pray for, encourage and financially support my role at ISMC), I noticed that the consulate returned *all* my submitted documents *except* the ones related to the ministry of ISMC!

People, this is no child's play. That fresh incident has been such a stark reminder of the reality of visa issues to 'restricted access countries' and why we should SO maximize the opportunity to lovingly and strategically reach the 100,000 Chinese international students (and tens of thousands of others) right here in our backyard in Canada alone! How foolish of us if we don't. God help us to *carpe diem!*

My use of India and China visa stories are particularly to illustrate how these are not the easiest countries to get into, but ironically are the ones which send the *most* international students to Canada and the United States; and are the top two countries with the most unreached people groups in the world. Need I say more?

3. No foreign language study

Errm...you don't have to learn another language to be a cross-cultural missionary? Since when?

I absolutely support and greatly admire missionaries who go to a strange place and spend years learning the language in order to share the

Gospel—especially when they have to translate the Scriptures, hitherto unheard in a mother tongue or heart language.

Remember, my point in this chapter is that the mission has never been easier. God, in an amazing twist, has brought hundreds of thousands of students across thousands of miles of sand and sea who are rather desperate to study and be communicated to in English!

No wonder people like Ted and Margaret, who for years have been running English as a Second Language (ESL) classes in our church basement have seen so much fruit! They actually use the Bible as the English textbook! And legitimately so! In fact, there's a lot of the English language and literature one may never get to really understand the root of until they've had some Biblical orientation.

Take for example the English expression, "scapegoat." One can never appreciate what a scapegoat is until he or she has read the book of Leviticus![156] Many of my ISMC staff reach out to international students through *teaching* ESL to be cross-cultural missionaries rather than having to be the ones *learning* Chinese, Korean, Farsi or some other language. The mission has never been easier!

4.   **Financially speaking**, many Christian businessmen, after hearing us cast this vision of reaching internationals right here, ask themselves: "so why aren't we doing more of this?!"

You'll have to forgive them for thinking the way they do—that is simply the mindset of a businessman: "How can I get more bang for my buck?" There is no more cost-effective way of doing global missions today than reaching internationals right among us.

When a good Canadian friend of mine and his family were posted to a Francophone African country, they had to spend a couple of years in France first, working on their French. Do you have any idea what the cost of living is in France? Now, you do the math!

After speaking at an event in Calgary, the province of Alberta's financial capital, one businessman "got it;" but there was a problem. He was angry. He was very upset because his own nephew had been conscripted to join a Christian campus ministry, undergone training, been deployed to China and eventually quit after two years. Over that period, a cool $200,000 had been invested in this venture.

Now this angry wise man was thinking: couldn't a fraction of that have been invested in an international student who is already here, who looks like his own and actually already speaks the language of the people he was going to be sent to in China? There are some one hundred thousand Chinese international students in Canada. Surely just one of them (0.001 percent) could do a better job than that, no?

5. No expertise or experience per se and you can be involved in global missions?

For sure! No one needs a degree in offering radical, unconditional love that shows itself in practical help to students from a foreign land?! Come on!

The era of us "professional" missionaries playing the game and asking the rest of the Body of Christ to watch us (and pay to watch us for that matter) is gone! Everyone can participate. Everyone *should* participate!

It is amazing how much of a 'family ministry' ISM can be. Everyone in a household—from children to grandparents—becomes a minister of sorts. And indeed, we ostensibly doing the ministry, get ministered to in significant ways too. As my British friend now living in South Africa, Emma Brewster, testifies, even as a child she herself was deeply ministered to and discipled through the life of an African international student her family hosted at their U.K. home. No wonder she's hooked for life to this ISM phenomenon. After working with international students in Britain, she has now moved to Cape Town to help pioneer ISM there and other places on the continent.

There are so many in the Body of Christ who really wanted to enlist in overseas mission, but for one reason or the other could not. Right where they are, with little or no expertise, they can be cross-cultural missionaries and ministers to the world that has come to their doorstep in such significant ways. Mission has never been easier!

6. Just Food, Fun, Friends, Fellowship?

They come to Christ by the dozen each year. There's hardly a month in which no one is being baptized at some partner church or the other, and yet this ultra-fruitful ministry is as simple as serving food and having fun.

As John Cudderford, my UBC Vancouver campus director, humorously puts it, almost without fail, these students who get saved will usually have a story that goes something like this: "I came for the food, I stayed for the friendship, and I eventually found faith!"

Can you just be a friend—something international students so greatly desire? Are you able to have fun? Do you like food? That's all! So you still don't believe the mission has never been easier?

ACRES OF DIAMONDS AND VINEYARDS

Do you remember Russell Conwell's famous story about the acres of diamonds? He is said to have told this story about five-thousand times while raising funds for the start of Temple University, which he founded.

The story is about a farmer who sold his land to go to a faraway place in search of diamonds that would make him rich. Needless to say, he never made it and committed suicide out of frustration. Meanwhile, back on his farm, the guy who bought it was casually strolling when he discovered these curious, tiny stones which turned out to be diamonds! And there were many!

The moral of the story is clear: the first farmer sold his farm which had acres of diamonds to go in search of what he already had. If only he had even taken the time to study what diamonds in the rough looked like!

Are we missing out on the "acres of diamonds" on our own soil, and going in search of 'lost people' at the ends of the earth? Pastor J.D. Payne of Alabama, whom I met in Toronto in 2014, and alluded to in Chapter Two, is spot on in his highly commended and recommended book, *Strangers Next Door:* "Something is missiologically malignant when we are willing to send people across the oceans, risking life and limb and spending enormous amounts of money, but we are not willing to walk next door and minister to the strangers living there."

I maintain that the mission has never been easier, and I'm certain that God has given us such low-hanging fruit that He must be frustrated at our leaves-much-to-be-desired realization and engagement.

In the fifth chapter of Isaiah's prophecies is a heart-breaking love song that God sings of His "acres of vines." He had intentionally found a fertile land, meticulously cleared it of stones and weeds, painstakingly tilled it, and planted the best species of the vine. He even protected it by fencing it and putting up a watchtower on the land. As if that were not enough, He added a winepress on site—no need to travel and hustle, even cutting the likelihood of post-harvest losses.

Then all He did was watch and wait for good grapes to come forth. Zero! Zip! Zilch! Nothing happened. Nada! Oh well, not quite. Something *did* happen. "Only bad fruit."

In frustration He croons like they do in a Nashville country music love song, *"What more could have been done for my vineyard than I have done for it?"*[157]

Really, you tell me: what more do we want God to do for us in our generation regarding closing the Great Commission? He's made cross-cultural missions so stunningly simple I wonder if any of us can dare ask for any more! If we are smart.

~11~

STRATEGICALLY SMART!

Out of this world!

*"Every soul is equally precious in God's sight,
but not every soul is equally strategic."*
~BILL BRIGHT

Whenever I consider this amazing phenomenon of international students, I can't help but say to the Lord, "You're soooo wise!" And I can't help but hear Him retort, "Duh?! What else do you expect?!"

No wonder if we do not walk with Him and take our marching orders from Him we are doing ourselves, and those we are to serve, a great disservice.

God never changes—"For I am the LORD, I change not"[158]—yet He's always doing new, "out-of-the-box" things: a new day, new season, new covenant, new testament, new heaven, a new earth, a new moon, new wine, new wineskin, new...you name it. He makes all things new!

To remind us just how "out of our box" His thinking and His ways are, God declares through the prophet Isaiah: "My thoughts are nothing like your thoughts," says the Lord. "And my ways are far beyond anything you could imagine. For just as the heavens are higher than the earth, so my ways are higher than your ways and my thoughts higher than your thoughts."[159]

Let me quickly show you three ways I find this ministry to international students such a strategically smart thing to do, only God could've thought of this. It's not just out of the box—it's literally out of this world!

I speak of:

1. Strategic Positioning
2. Strategic Picture window (frame)
3. Strategic People.

1. STRATEGIC POSITIONING

Shocking as it may be, less than 2.7 percent of the 1.84 billion global emerging generation (under 14s) could be considered to have come from a protestant evangelical Christian background.[160]

So what does this ultra-smart God decide to do about this? "No problem where they are born," He muses. "It is what it is." But then He strategizes, knowing beforehand that, before long, these young people would be itching to get a Western experience and degree. So, "I'll bring them to you in North America where I've strategically positioned you—show them my love and share with them my Gospel. Deal?" Deal, Lord! Deal! How very strategic! Totally out of this world!

KONICHIWA! WAKE UP!

This was exactly Kenji's story—who really is a perfect prototype of how this God-strategy works. I have had the joy of meeting so many of the people that hosted and helped this young man, Kenji Kondo, who found Christ in

Canada, having come from a Buddhist home in Japan. Lailani Mendoza[161] tells Kenji's background best:[162]

It's the biggest complaint people have about Christians. To some people, Christians are simply hypocrites—people who pretend to be pure and holy, yet upon stepping outside of the church, switch gears and are back to worldly, sinful living. Sometimes, it's just a result of others' biases but at other times, unfortunately, the observation is accurate.

Kenji was one of those observers. Growing up in rural Japan, Kenji was born and raised in a strong Buddhist family and barely had any contact with other people that weren't Buddhists.

"I never met a Christian person until high school," he said. "I hated anybody who was religious for some reason, especially Christians. I thought Christians were hypocrites."

While children from Christian families would usually spend their summers in Vacation Bible Schools, Kenji's were spent in a Shinto temple, learning incantations that would be so ingrained in his memory he would still remember them many years later into adulthood.

"Even though I was surrounded by all those rituals, I grew up to become an atheist." Instead, he pursued a hedonistic lifestyle while working in bars and night clubs.

Later, an opportunity came for Kenji to continue his education in Canada—a move that would create a paradigm shift in his life.

"I was 20 years old when I came to Canada," he said, reliving the past. "I couldn't speak English when I came. I had a real hard time adjusting to living in this country." For the first time, he was in the most vulnerable stage of his life. Yet God chose this perfect moment for Kenji to revisit his old biases.

"In my first year of living in Canada, all six host families I stayed with were Christians. Although I thought they were fools for believing in God, at the same time they were useful to me. They were more patient with my English and showed interest in my life. And because their religion prohibited them from cheating me or lying to me, I knew I could trust them."

When Kenji moved to Calgary to study ESL, he stayed in the house of Danny and Elma Kroeker, the couple who started a FOCUS[163] club in the city. Still, Kenji's worldly pursuits got the better of him: "Every Friday, FOCUS was held at their house—my house! I met a lot of nice people at FOCUS. But when they had Bible study, I chose to go to a bar and dance with girls instead."

What did get through to Kenji was a Japanese evangelist who spoke at the church he was attending years later.

"He was a former Japanese Yakuza mafia for 17 years before he got saved. He is now an outstanding evangelist. He spoke at an American presidential prayer breakfast with Billy Graham and led a *March for Jesus* from the northern tip to the southern end of Japan."

"When I heard his testimony, I couldn't deny the power of God but believe Him. As soon as I believed in Jesus, everything I had heard about God and the message from the Bible made sense. I thought, "I attended church for almost four years. How come I didn't understand this truth before?"

"In the book of Acts, chapter 9, when Ananias healed Paul's eyes, something like scales came off from his eyes. A Japanese idiom, 'scales came off my eyes' means a person came to understand something that he didn't formerly understand. It was like that for me. It was like a veil was taken off my eyes so that I could see what God was saying all these years."

After becoming a Christian, he met and married a Canadian girl from FOCUS who worked with International Student Ministries Canada (ISMC). Now, Kenji works for Wycliffe Bible Translators in Japan.

UPROOTING FIVE HUNDRED YEARS OF OCCULTIC HISTORY

Today, Kenji and his Canadian wife Sandy are back in Japan and making an impact for the Kingdom as full-time workers with Wycliffe Bible Translators. Can you imagine what their presence and impact is doing to the one percent Christian statistic in Japan?

In March 2014, I was getting ready to speak at a banquet in Calgary when I received an email. My heart was so dearly warmed. I hadn't realized that, not only had Kenji been saved, but his household also. His Dad was now saved and recently baptized! Hallelujah!

With Kenji's kind permission I will share portions of his March 29 email (unedited) with you:

> After my Dad's baptism, he went ahead on removing our family's membership from the Buddhist temple as well as quit the deacon's role. To removing the membership, he had to sign a paper to terminate the existing relationship with the temple. Because my father (along with the Buddhist monk's family) is a direct **descendant of the samurai** who came to start this village in **late 1500's**, he was the caretaker of some of the gravestones of ancestors.

On March 25, because my Dad was unable to go, **Sandy and I represented our family** at Syonenuki done by the Buddhist priest. Syonenuki is a ceremony to take the spirit out of the stones so that a mason can come in to remove the stones.

As the monk started the ceremony, his hand was **trembling**. The shake became so bad that he had difficulty placing the incense on the ground. Even while chanting, his hands continued to tremble. Sandy thought that there was a **spiritual battle** taking place because of our presence (with the Holy Spirit). We prayed to the true & living God as the monk chanted. We want you to know that your prayers for us are at the forefront of the battle here.

Incense was placed in front of each stone, and the monk chanted incantations. These were the same incantations that Kenji memorized by heart when he was young. The sound of chanting and the incense was a powerful agent to bring back memories of his childhood Buddhist worship. The Monk then placed the mound of salt on each stones before rebuking the spirits and commanding them to not to harm people for removing the stones. The **fear of spiritual curses** are very real to Japanese people. But we believe in the powerful protection from the Holy Spirit, and the true and living God who raised Jesus Christ from the dead.

Inari shrine is gone!

Inari is one of the few Japanese gods that has a different history from the rest of the Shinto gods. Its biggest shrine, called **Fushimi-Inari**, (located in Kyoto, 85 km west of

145

here) covers an entire mountain. Years ago, **my grand-ma's sister** trained herself in Fushimi-Inari and became an **Itako** (see the explanation below), and brought home an Inari shrine. When her family deceased, my father Hatsuo inherited the shrine. So we had an Inari shrine within our house compound as long as I have lived. After the baptism, my father with the help of my Mom, **removed the shrine** from our compound.

I know missionaries in Japan who have toughed it out for nearly two decades and not seen much visible fruit (of course we know God may still be at work) but God picks one Japanese who comes to Canada ostensibly to get a Canadian degree, and totally changes a Japanese household, back in Asia?

Do you see God's strategic positioning? He orchestrates the perfect stage of life, the right city, campus and country, the perfect time period, the right inner and external conditions, and bam! This is the story of many an international student—the strategic positioning of God. Out of this world!

2. STRATEGIC PICTURE WINDOW

Remember I alluded to Luis Bush's 10/40 Window at the Lausanne II Conference in Manila? Well, since 1989 this region of the world has been the major focus of Christian missionary activity, especially as we engage in "frontier mission," going where no one has ever gone because it's "too remote," "so restricted," "too dangerous," or whatever.

There has been a lot of focus on the 10/40 Window for many reasons. I like the brow-raising, vivid picture window view "win1040.com" gives:

> The 10/40 Window is located from 10 degrees to 40 degrees north of the equator. There are 69 nations across northern Africa, the Middle East and Central Asia in the 10/40 Window. Nearly 4 billion people live here, including 90 percent of the world's poorest of the poor. It is estimated that 1.6 billion of these people have never had the chance to hear the Gospel of Jesus Christ—not even once! The seat of every major non-Christian religion—Islam, Buddhism, Hinduism, Animism, Atheism, and Sikhism—is headquartered in the 10/40 Window. Two-thirds of the world's population (4 billion) live in the 69 nations of the 10/40 Window.

- Two-thirds of the world's population—4 billion people—live in the 10/40 Window.
- 95% of these 4 billion people are unevangelized.
- 87% are the poorest of the poor, living on an average of only $250 per family annually.
- In many of the 69 nations, witnessing the Christian Gospel is illegal and will result in imprisonment or death.
- 45 of the 50 worst countries in the world for persecution of Christians are in the 10/40 Window.
- Child prostitution and child slavery run rampant in many of these nations.
- Horrific abuse of women and children remains unchecked, including an epidemic of pedophilia.

- A majority of the world's terrorist organizations are based in the 10/40 Window, and children as young as 18 months old are trained to be Jihad soldiers.[164]

THINKING OUTSIDE THE WINDOW

This is pretty serious stuff. So imagine all the seriousness with which I'm taking my prayer for this window as a newbie-missionary (at least officially; since I believe I've always been a missionary of sorts), when all of a sudden God totally twists my thinking and whispers: "But Yaw, *I am thinking outside the window!*" Whaaat?! Who in their right mind will think *outside* this strategic window?! Out of this world!

And so I quickly go rampaging through research materials to understand what the Lord is saying and then I finally get it. What He meant to tell me was that He's pulled the brightest and the best *out of the window* and placed them right in our backyards, whether in the Western world or elsewhere, to reach out to with the love, lives, lips, and literature of the Gospel and send them back into the Window for godly transformation!

You won't believe my findings among the sending countries of international students to Canada:[165]

- The **top four** are *all* in the 10/40 Window.
- These are China—the stronghold of Buddhism and Atheism; India—the stronghold of Hinduism; South Korea (similar picture as China, in spite of significant growth of Christianity), and Saudi Arabia—the stronghold of Islam.
- These top four constitute more than half (54.29 percent) of all the international students in Canada, equaling 159,355 students.
- Apart from the United States, Mexico, and France, *all* the **top ten** sending countries to Canada are in the window: China, India, South Korea, Saudi Arabia, Japan, Nigeria, and Iran.

- These seven nations in the 10/40 Window represent 176,550 of international students, or 61.98 percent of all international students in Canada!

Time and space do not allow me to tell you story after story of how literally thousands of people, still in the window, have been saved because of their relatives (not just students) who God brought here "out of the window!" *Thinking outside the window,* indeed!

STRATEGICALLY-SMART thing to do

Thus saith the Lord:
"I AM thinking outside the window!"
2/3 of the world's population

Number of international students in Canada (2013) from the top four sending countries—all from the 10/40 Window

A WAY IN THE WILDERNESS

Do you remember the old Don Moen classic that went, *"God will make a way where there seems to be no way; He works in ways we cannot see, He will make a way for me..."*?

Well, as I think about the 10/40 Window (Christians originally called it "the resistant belt") and how it still is such a great challenge today, God's strategy revealed to us in "thinking outside the window" so much resonates with the prophecy of Isaiah: "See, I am doing a new thing! Now it springs up; do you not perceive it? I am making a way in the desert and streams in the wasteland."[166]

The very places we said were hard and dangerous to reach, God says to the Church, "Hey, I've made a way" in those harsh deserts and treacherous wastelands. But again, He calls us to *"See!" Open our eyes and look!* Or else if we use yesterday's spectacles, thinking *inside* the box or window, we will miss it...or worse, we will miss Him! Do you perceive it?

COUNT 402

"It has always been my ambition to preach the Gospel where Christ was not known, so that I would not be building on someone else's foundation."[167]

If Paul's ambition had been ours too, perhaps we would've been done with the Great Commission by now! For a long time, it seems the majority of the Body of Christ has been spinning its wheels. This is what I mean: *97-99 percent of our missionaries and mission dollars are sent to places that have already been reached with the Gospel,* according to *The Issachar Initiative.*[168]

So ISMC is committing to be part of *The Issachar Initiative* which wants to "Count for Zero:" zero languages without the Scriptures (4,000 don't have); zero people groups without disciple makers (3,000 don't); zero people who have not heard the Gospel (3.5 billion haven't); zero villages or neighborhoods without a church (1 million have none).

As far as I am concerned, international students per se are an "unreached people group" in Canada. Also, the majority of them come from the countries with the most unreached people groups in the world, notably India and China. These two countries have the most numbers of unreached people groups in the world! And they are right here! As we have seen, way more than 60 percent of these international students come from the least reached and most resistant areas of the world: the 10/40 Window.

We did define an unreached people group in Chapter One, but what does it mean to call a group not just unreached but *unengaged*? An *unengaged people group* means there is no known disciple-maker or missionary committed to reach that group for Christ. Four of the top ten countries with the most unengaged, unreached people groups in the world[169] are among the top ten countries with the most international students in Canada: India, China, Saudi Arabia and France.

For real? Yet *they walk among us*—the people we are trying to reach are here and looking for us! Both the harvest and the harvesters are here!

At ISMC, we want to "Count for Zero" *too*, count for [4] zero [0] too [2] (Count 402). Our *big dream is that in the next decade* **zero** *international students in Canada will return to their countries unreached by the Body of Christ.* And that ultimately this will translate to *zero* unreached people groups in the world within the next ten to twenty years.

Again those stinging words of J.D. Payne, *"Something is missiologically malignant when we are willing to send people across the oceans, risking life and limb and spending enormous amounts of money, but we are not willing to walk next door and minister to the strangers living there."*

PICTURE PERFECT

Toward the end of the year I got wind that a young international student who had just graduated from Peace River Bible Institute in Alberta wanted to do an internship with ISMC. I jumped at the opportunity. I had been praying for a younger leader who could come alongside me in ministry, life and leadership; one I could pour into.

I love working with young people and have a passion for raising emerging leaders, so you can understand why I jumped at the opportunity. But you wouldn't believe just how high I jumped. Pretty high. You know why? This young man was a rare Christian from Pakistan, smack in the 10/40 Window.

Just to give you an idea how serious business this is: of Pakistan's 447 people groups, 435 of them are considered unreached (i.e. less than 2 percent evangelical Christian). Only 0.7 percent of the 184,582,000 are Christian adherents (we can't tell exactly how many are actually evangelicals). It goes without saying that the largest religious group in Pakistan is Islam (98.9 percent).[170]

Who in their right mind wouldn't want to love Shahzad, train and mentor him *outside the window* to send him back into the window for God? Would we rather he be influenced by some radical suicide-bombing-thinking Jihadists of the Talibanic order lurking in the dark streets of downtown Toronto or Calgary? God forbid!

And that brings me to the third reason why it is so strategically smart to reach out to these international students.

3. STRATEGIC PEOPLE

Newsflash: the *brightest and best* from the 10/40 Window and all over the world are here!

Not too long ago I was in a church out somewhere in Western Canada to preach, as I often have the privilege of doing. Round about that time the new North Korean Supreme Leader, Kim Jung Un, had reportedly killed eighty people for watching smuggled television broadcasts and possibly wielding Bibles.[171]

Quite understandably, the church was in an uproar as the congregation lifted prayers to God Almighty to intervene. Anyone who knows me will tell you I believe in prayer. If I didn't, I wouldn't be up at four in the morning to seek God's face. Yet right about the start of this fervent prayer being lifted,

I heard a soft divine voice whisper to me: "But he was an international student!" Indeed, for some time he studied in Switzerland.

I just can't help but wonder, "What if?" What if when this young man was studying in Switzerland a Christian who "gets it" had spotted him and loved him, befriended him, and shared the Gospel with him. What if?

YOUTHPOWER!™

In 2004, I introduced a revolutionary paradigm which has now gone global: *Youth Power!*™ This double-edged movement simultaneously seeks to get society to stop and pay attention to "the most influential people on earth," Young People, and also start a fire in these very Young People for them to recognize their purpose and potential, get their act together and do something significant with their lives...and NOW!

Throughout the history of the world, God has used Young People more than any other demographic as change agents and guess what? The strategic people we speak of right now, international students, are mainly Young People.

Consider the sheer **numbers** (there are more Young People on earth than ever before in the history of the world), **control** (think of the Arab Spring), **influence**, **strength** and **energy**, **special abilities** (talents), **creativity** and raw **passion** of this demographic. We are sitting on gold, a great global force for good or ill! Strategic people indeed!

THE NEXT CHAPTER

Where are the next world leaders? They are mainly in our universities and colleges right now! Dr. Charles Malik, who once served as president of the United Nations General Assembly and Security Council once said, "The university is a clear-cut fulcrum with which to move the world. More potently than by any other means, change the university and you change the world."

I think of the Chinese *international scholar* (not everyone comes as an undergrad or graduate student, some come as post-docs, visiting scholars, etc.) who found Christ while doing research in Canada. He returned to continue his career as dean of a university with over 100,000 engineering students under his influence. He, not too long ago, led his brother, a politician in the Communist government, to the Lord.

It was Billy Graham who said, "You might be the person that God uses to bring the next world leader into a personal relationship with Jesus Christ." How strategic!

"ALL FINGERS ARE NOT EQUAL"

All fingers are fingers, made of flesh and bone and blood. Each one is important, but in the Akan language from Ghana, my mother tongue, we have a profound saying which translates as, "All fingers are not equal." Such folk wisdom came to light more than ever in my anatomy class in medical school when I learnt how totally indispensable the THUMB is!

I still remember Prof. C.N.B. Tagoe in his element at the basic science auditorium of the University of Ghana Medical School, speaking with glee about the anatomy of the opposable thumbs of humans. The thumb is the shortest, thickest digit on the human hand and moves in a different direction than the other digits. It is called opposable because the thumb can be moved around to touch the other fingers, which gives people the ability to grasp things.

Most primates (humans, apes, monkeys) and some other animals have opposable thumbs. Humans can move their thumb farther across their hand than any other primate. Having opposable thumbs helps in grasping things more easily, picking up small objects, and eating with one's hand, not just for those of us from cultures who eat directly with the hand, but even for holding any kind of cutlery. So all fingers are important indeed, but "all fingers are not equal."

Where am I going with this? I will be the last to be condescending to any ministry or expression of gifts, being a strong believer and teacher of unique, God-given purpose. Having said that, not all ministries are the same; all are not equally strategic. And quite honestly, if I didn't find the ministry of ISMC to be strategic, I wouldn't give my life to it! Don't forget I died in 2008, and I'm living on borrowed time. I have no time to waste on non-strategic things (of no eternal value for that matter)!

I must confess that the first time I read *"Every soul is equally precious in God's sight, but not every soul is equally strategic"* attributed to Campus Crusade for Christ founder Bill Bright, I paused and thought, "Hmm, that sounds like heresy!" I never got the chance to meet Dr. Bright in person, but I bless God for the opportunity to meet Vonette, his dear surviving wife, a couple of times in the Lausanne circles.

After much pondering, I finally understood what Bill meant. You see, every single soul is important to God, equally precious such that if there was only one person on earth, God would've *still* sent Jesus to die! That being said—and permit me to use one of my investment world terms here—not every soul will give the same ROI (Return on Investment) in terms of earthly and eternal impact.

On the Day of Pentecost, after Peter's anointed speech, 3,000 came to faith. Yet in my mind (and God knows my mind is very limited) none of those 3,000 may have been as strategic in replicating and spreading the Gospel like that one convert on the Damascus road—Paul. We easily owe half of the work and the books of the New Testament to him! Each of these 3,001 souls are equally precious in God's sight but not equally strategic.

The story of Philip and the Ethiopian Eunuch in Acts 8 so typifies how "strategic people" are top of God's list in His dealings with humankind.

PHILIP'S PROJECT

Imagine you were Philip, frontier missionary, breaking grounds in Samaria for the first time since Jesus left (don't forget, that up until now, when persecution broke out after the death of Stephen, the disciples of Jesus had basically kept the Gospel to the Jewish people and territories). Philip was among the first to break through cross-culturally.

He was having a blast in Samaria: *"When the CROWDS heard Philip and saw the signs he performed, they all paid close attention to what he said. For with shrieks, impure spirits came out of many, and many who were paralyzed or lame were healed. So there was great joy in that city." ...when they believed Philip as he proclaimed the good news of the kingdom of God and the name of Jesus Christ, they were baptized, both men and women."*[172] (emphasis mine)

Even a long-time PhD in sorcery called Simon, believed and was baptized. This was such a great evangelistic campaign that HQ was radioed to come in and see, and bless the people with the Holy Spirit. Archbishops Peter and John themselves, of Jesus' original dozen, came.

Then, instead of the all-important work of "follow up" of the crowds saved (or more revival programs for the masses), God calls Philip out of the *crowds* to go after one guy, just *one guy*! One guy on a lonely desert road heading towards Africa. And he was Black! Why? *He was strategic.* As an influential man, finance minister of Ethiopia, he would go back and be the beginning of the Church in his nation!

We've already established that *it is God who moves people* (people movements are God movements): "Now an angel of the LORD said to Philip, **"RISE AND GO** toward the south to the road that goes down from Jerusalem to Gaza."[173] "And **he ROSE and WENT**."[174] (emphasis added) Meanwhile in the same verse we realize that God had also *moved* this Ethiopian government official (treasurer of Queen Candace) to travel from Africa to Jerusalem to worship and was returning home to Ethiopia in his chariot. Again, "and the Spirit said to Philip, "**GO OVER** and JOIN THIS CHARIOT.""[175] (emphasis added)

So while God moved the finance minister across his border to get to know His name, He simultaneously moved Philip to get to spread His fame. I can't help but notice it was God Himself who brought Philip and the Ethiopian together. But again, I can't help noticing that this man was returning home without having understood the Gospel—without being saved. I wonder how many such strategic people return to the 10/40 Window today, or wherever they came from, without ever being approached by a Christ-follower.

Like many internationals—new immigrants, refugees, or international students—you would notice that the Ethiopian was *curious but confused*. It may be the culture, food, slang, or weather. Many times, when we have engaged them enough to get into the Scriptures, it is the Bible itself they may have questions about, just like this eunuch. He was reading Isaiah. Philip showed interest and he reciprocated: "*[30]So Philip ran to him and heard him reading Isaiah the prophet and asked, "Do you understand what you are reading?"[31]And he said, "How can I, unless someone guides me?" And he invited Philip to come up and sit with him.*"[176]

This is a key verse: "*Then Philip opened his mouth, and **beginning with this scripture he told him the good news about Jesus.***"[177] (emphasis mine) That is God for you! He meets people where they're at! *"Beginning with this scripture."* Just like in Jesus' encounter with the Samaritan woman, where He began with a conversation about the practical issue at hand—water—which was her *felt* need. From there He proceeded to offer the *real* water—salvation.

Paul did the same thing when he went to Athens (in Acts 17), where he saw an altar with an intriguing inscription. He began his address thus: "*People of Athens! I see that in every way you are very religious. For as I walked around and looked carefully at your objects of worship, I even found an altar with this inscription: TO AN UNKNOWN GOD. So you are ignorant of the very thing you worship*—**and this is what I am going to proclaim to you.**"[178] (emphasis in bold added)

The interesting thing is that the latter part of this same speech is where God reveals that He determines the exact places where people should reside so that they might reach out to Him and find Him!

God strategically meets strategic people where they're at—taking care of their immediate and felt needs (what they are doing and seeking). For international students:

- *What they are doing* is mainly studying so help with things like ESL classes, English conversation practice, reviewing/correction of papers, practical job skills training, professional mentorship etc.
- *What they are seeking* is genuine friendship, fun (want to explore the new country and experience its culture), family (home away from home), food etc. Remember the resounding theme? *"I came for the food, I stayed for the friendship, and I found faith."*

The Ethiopian publically expressed his faith through water baptism just as many of these internationals do. At ISMC we witnessed about fifty such between the summers of 2013 and 2014 alone. Praise the Lord!

So if God is *strategically* positioning *strategic* people from and to the *strategic* picture window, should the least we could do not be to get a bit more *strategic ourselves* about how we engage them?

PART III:

DON'T GET BOXED IN

*The conventional view serves to protect us
from the painful job of thinking.*
~ JOHN KENNETH GALBRAITH

*Man's mind stretched to a new idea never
goes back to its original dimension.*
~ OLIVER WENDELL HOLMES

~12~

Easy Ministry or
Strategic Ministry?

***Box deliveries—the right stuff to the right people
at the right time in the right places***

*"The world can no longer be left to mere diplomats, politicians and business
leaders. They have done the best they could, no doubt. But this is an age for
spiritual heroes—a time for men and women to be heroic in their faith and
in spiritual character and power. The greatest danger to the Christian church
today is that of pitching its message too low."*
~Dallas Willard

S cottish missionary James Gilmour, in sharing why he decided on
heading to Mongolia of all the possible things he could do and places
in the world he could go, basically said, "Because it was most strategic." Hear
him: *"I thought it reasonable that I should seek the work where the work was
the most abundant and the workers fewest."* It may not have been the easiest,

but that was okay, so long as what he was doing would give him "the most bang for his buck."

EVEN ME!

Every winter, as my tropical family and I shiver and shuffle through the snow, I ask myself: "What on earth am I doing here?!" "Why did you move to Canada?" is one of my most frequently asked questions. Sometimes when I'm in a naughty mood I answer, "For the weather." Quite frankly, but for divine purpose, I wouldn't endure these winters for anything.

My point? It's not everything we do because it's easy; there are some things we simply engage in because they are strategic. If at this particular point in our lives, the Lord finds it strategic that my family be in the West and close to the North Pole for His strategic purposes—so be it.

If we would work hard at investing in these international students, who are invariably the brightest and best from their nations, we will be shocked just how much of a multiplier effect we would see. Are we going to remain content feeding them for free on Friday nights over hearty conversations about countries and cultures, or should we be looking at being a bit more strategic in our engagement with them?

DISTRESS CALL FROM MEXICO

"Help Doctor..." were the words from the other end of the phone line. Did I hear right? He was far away in Mexico. Manuel and I met at one Saturday morning leadership training session I facilitated at Peoples Church of Montreal. We hit it off and a friendship and mentorship began. We would even meet at a McDonald's to catch up on life.

Manuel was a postgraduate (Master's) engineering student who had come to McGill University for a couple of semesters as part of his program. All too soon the time came for Manuel to return to Mexico. I voluntarily and heartily went to pick him up from his residence that early morning and dropped him off at the airport after committing him into the Lord's hands and informally commissioning him for impact.

A couple of months later I got a distress call. That call. It was Manuel. What could it be? He was asking for help. No, not asking for money, I hope. Manuel said, "Help Doctor, I'm leading my boss!" I had never heard anything quite like that, but because of our shared leadership lingua I got what he was trying to say.

Manuel had become so *functionally* efficacious and instrumental since he went back to Mexico that he was influencing his own *positional* leader at work, "leading my boss." Manuel wanted some more leadership training for the next level. Even his own youth pastor in Mexico had begun to look to him for leadership.

So we resumed leadership training sessions via Skype—something I've been engaged in for other emerging leaders in Singapore, China, England, and Australia—and after a while, handed him over to one of my trained associates in the United States.

And the story has just begun, act one, scene one. But what if all I had been content to do was meet up and chat up—the easy thing to do—and never gone that extra mile to teach and develop him as an emerging leader (the strategic thing to do)?

BLESSING TRICKLING OR BOMB TICKING?

Once I met a former executive of the American Bible Society (ABS). This was in the lobby of a hotel in Budapest, where we both had come for a Lausanne leaders meeting. The year was 2007.

He was so enthusiastic in his greeting of me when he realized I was Ghanaian. According to him, the largest order for Bibles in the history of the ABS was in his era when the then-president of Ghana, Dr. Kwame

Nkrumah, ordered five hundred thousand copies of the Bible for distribution in Ghanaian schools.[179]

For me, this gesture by the highest office in that newly independent African state came from one who had come full circle. Kwame Nkrumah had not long before been an international student in Pennsylvania. While it is hard to tell whether Kwame Nkrumah had personal faith in the Lord Jesus Christ, it is documented that during his time in the United States, Nkrumah preached at Black Presbyterian churches in Philadelphia and New York City.

Kwame Nkrumah got into political activity even as an international student in the USA and England and eventually became the first President and Prime Minister of Ghana after wrestling the Gold Coast out of the hands of the British colonial powers. While lecturing in political science at his alma mater, Lincoln University, he was elected president of the African Students Organization of America and Canada.[180]

It was when he later went to England to pursue law that he met the famous pan-Africanist, George Padmore, and together worked to organize the fifth Pan-African Congress in Manchester. Subsequently, Nkrumah founded the West African National Secretariat to work towards the decolonization of Africa, in addition to his role as vice-president of the West African Students Union (WASU).[181] Many of Nkrumah's African international student contemporaries in the West were the agitators of independence and founding fathers of the new African states, including Jomo Kenyatta of Kenya and Nnamdi Azikiwe of Nigeria.

While Nkrumah was an international student, he studied some theology—after graduating with a bachelor's in 1939 he also received an STB (bachelor of sacred theology) from Lincoln three years later. Of course Kwame Nkrumah was no angel, he was far from perfect, yet I can't help but contrast the historical Bible-ordering and Bible-distributing president with the current North Korean Supreme Leader, Kim Jung Un, who reportedly kills Bible-wielding Koreans! Both of them were international students; the latter in Switzerland.

Whichever way you look at it, international students are emerging leaders, with the destinies of nations in their hands, literally.

MORDECAIS AND MIDWIVES

One of my major mandates as president of ISMC is to engender a mindset, search for and test syllabi, processes and best practices for *intentional* leadership development of these emerging leaders. Incidentally, I was the plenary speaker for ISMC's 2013 National Staff Conference themed on Student Leadership Development. This was arranged with my predecessor, way before any talks of becoming ISMC president ever surfaced.

With all the gusto I could gather, I poured my heart out to the staff about how critical it is not just to do easy ministry, but strategic ministry. In other words, are we just going to befriend and have fun with these students or are we going to get serious about speaking into their lives and mentoring them, like Mordecai did for the emerging leader Esther, for the eternal salvation of their people groups and earthly prosperity of their geopolitical nations?

Whether needing to be delivered out of boxes of obscurity (like the womb of potential) or pulled out of their shells (boxes) into which they have reclined out of the extremes of lack of self-confidence on one hand or a sense of entitlement on the other rather than a keen sense of purpose to serve their generation, these fledgling leaders need midwives and Mordecais to facilitate their emergence.

One of our staff, originally from Singapore, kept saying "Thank you!" "Thank you for changing my mindset about how I see these students." And indeed, I had rather sternly told my staff, "Please stop calling them *kids*!" These students are *emerging leaders*; not kids. "These present students are the leaders who are going to determine the kind of world in which you retire!"

Some staff have really caught it; others are struggling to. Some sister ministries to international students don't even see what I'm talking about.

They are unable to think outside their half-a-century-old window (paradigm). Others are innovatively running with the vision, full speed!

CAMBODIA, HERE I COME!

With time, the fruit each bears will show. My heart was so warmed when one of my leading staff, who really gets it, said on the phone (from across the country), how just deciding to begin the conversation about intentional leadership development with one student shocked him into reality.

Apparently this student from Cambodia, who perhaps had been seen as a 'kid' all this while, has a father who is in government in Cambodia and this chap knew he was invariably going back into a government position after returning to the country.

It suddenly dawned on my city director, "I have nine months to make a leader out of him." "Well, all the best" I said, chuckling. Come to think of it, nine months' gestation is all God needs to form a baby from a seed at conception to a full-grown baby ready for delivery. But then once the child is born, he has the rest of his lifetime to grow, right?

When a group of Intervarsity USA leaders and I had a chat about this during the Association of Christians Ministry among Internationals (ACMI) Conference in Columbus, Ohio, in 2013, they got it. In fact, they so got it that they invited me to speak to their staff, who were gathering in St. Louis, Missouri, in January 2014 about this.

I remember one staff member writing to me afterwards and saying what really captured his heart was the challenge I threw to them to see themselves as *midwives*. "You must see yourselves as midwives, overseeing the process of birthing leaders who are going to change the world by Jesus Christ!"

WHY MORE RAFIKIS NEEDED

Disney's "Lion King" remains my favorite animated movie of all time. I mean the original, not the sequels. Do you remember how Simba, though he was born to be king, had lost his sense of purpose and direction (thanks to farting Pumba and precocious Timone); just content with the "Hakuna matata" life of "no worries?"

When he began the road back to discovering who he was and what he was born to be, Simba was fortunate to have the wise old sage of a monkey, Rafiki, mercilessly knock the young lion's head with his staff, bringing him out of his stupor, and graciously say, "Follow Rafiki, he knows the way!"

Whenever I've visited the beautiful land of Kenya, I quite ashamedly haven't been able to communicate beyond the rudimentary "hi," "bye," and "thank you" in Swahili, but my Kenyan friends tell me "Rafiki" in Swahili means "friend."

Many of these students don't even see the leader in themselves. They need a Rafiki who will come alongside and point them to the leaders they are, albeit in an embryonic state, and guide them along the path towards taking their place in their generation to lead the nations.

In a response to the proposal that we need to teach leadership to these students, one of my HuD Group-trained leadership coaches and ISMC ministry partner in Montreal, Celine Matteau, wrote back with the following feedback (after inviting international students to her home and having a good time with them):

> *"The students are interested in meeting again for other activities (including food) and are willing to be contacted personally or by invitation via Facebook."*

> *"Leadership did not seem to be relevant to them because they associate leadership with management in the secular world."*

"The students are presently in science programs. They are more interested in learning the technical aspects of work."

We have our work cut out for us!

THE TENSION

The same God has made ISM both stunningly simple and strategically significant. Those who are able to skillfully handle that tension of easy ministry versus strategic ministry will win the day. To the Irish-American novelist and short story writer, Francis Scott Fitzgerald, "The test of a first rate intelligence is the ability to hold two opposed ideas in the mind at the same time, and still retain the ability to function."

I bet we would do ministry differently if we knew *for sure* that a certain international student was going to become:

- Belize Prime Minister: George C. Prize
- Cyprus President: George Vasiliou
- Ecuador President: Sixto Duran
- Ghana Prime Minister: Kwame Nkrumah
- Ghana President: Edward Akufo-Addo
- Ghana Prime Minister: Kofi Abrefa Busia
- Ghana President: Hilla Limann
- Ghana President: John Agyekum Kuffuor
- Ghana President: John Evans Atta Mills

(Clear bias but every single one of Ghana's substantive, democratic heads of state since becoming an independent nation in 1957 has been an international student, except two)

- Ireland President: Mary Robinson
- Israel Prime Minister: Benjamin Netanyahu
- Ivory Coast Prime Minister: Alassan Ouatarra
- Japan Princess: Masako Owado
- Jordan Prime Minister: Tahir al-Masri
- Liberia President: Charles Taylor
- Mexico President: Carlos Salinas
- New Zealand Governor-General: Geoffrey Palmer
- Nicaragua President: Violeta Barrios de Chamorro
- Philippines President: Corazon Aquino
- Singapore's *first* Prime Minister: Lee Kuan Yew
- Singapore's *second* Prime Minister: Goh Chok Tong
- Singapore's *third* (and current) Prime Minister: Lee Hsien Loong

(Essentially, all of Singapore's Prime Ministers were once international students)

- Sudan SPLA Rebel Leader: John Garang
- Sweden Prime Minister: Ingvar Carlsson
- Taiwan Premier: Lein Chan
- Taiwan President: Lee Teng-hui
- Turkey Prime Minister: Tansu Ciller
- First modern woman Muslim leader, 11th Prime Minister of Pakistan: Benazir Bhutto.

What if each had had a serious Rakifi who was a Christ-follower and leader-developer when they were international students? "Imagine watching the news in ten years' time and finding out to your shock that the latest 'leader' in Africa or Asia was one of your own students whom you befriended and even 'discipled,' but never taught an iota of leadership," I challenge ISM staff.

Let me state right here and now that I strongly believe that if we had discipled people as thoroughly and completely as Jesus Christ did his followers during His earthly sojourn, we wouldn't be needing to distinguish 'discipleship' from 'leadership development' today. In the same way, there can be no proper leadership development without the character and spiritual formation that discipleship entails. Be that as it may, in this era it has become important to clearly and distinctly state both terms in order to ensure that nothing about the formation of the head, heart and hands of emerging leaders falls through the cracks.

And by the way, the list above is only the tip of the iceberg of world leaders who have been international students mainly in North America and a handful in Europe, not counting other places of study and other spheres of endeavor beyond governance!

According to ISMC, this, then, is how a complete cycle of strategic engagement with these emerging leaders should look like:

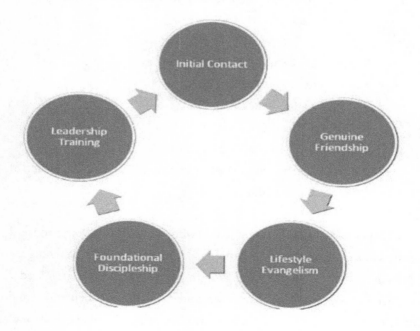

CREATION CRIES

Look everywhere in the world, every continent and region, every segment of life, every sector of the economy and there is a cry for help! The need for godly, effective servant leadership has never been greater.

I am very much aware of the eschatological reading of the eighth chapter of Paul's epistle to the people of Rome. I can't help but notice, however, that the cry of *all* creation (from archeology to zoology) is for godly, effectual servant leaders to rise up and take care of issues.

These international students are global solutions for global problems and the whole world waits in eager expectation, groaning, as in the pains of childbirth right up to this moment, for children of God (the ultimate Leader and Problem-solver) to be revealed.[182] Cancer awaits, HIV/AIDS, too. Not just the unmedicated, the unfed. The billion people with untreated water, the millions who are uneducated. Need I go on?

The manifestation of these emerging leaders is three-dimensional, '3D' literally:

1. *Desired*~the creation desires it[183]
2. *Demanded*~the Creator demands it[184]
3. *Dreaded*~the devil dreads it.[185]

CHURCH CRIETH

Even the Church has not been left out of this leadership crisis either. In fact, statistics show that there are teeming numbers coming to Christ *every day*, especially in the Global South, than there are leaders being produced to plant churches, lead communities of faith, disciple people and raise more leaders (see EQUIP's graph below).

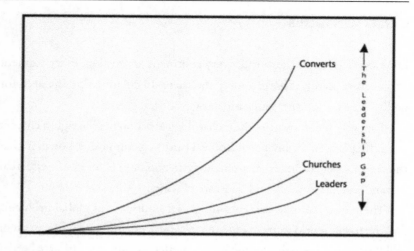

Credit: EQUIP, Leadership Notebook One

COLEMAN'S COUNSEL

So whether it's creation's cry or the church's, the temptation is to jump in there and solve the gross problems of the masses. But that wasn't Jesus' approach, and that shouldn't be ours either. Feeding the masses, per se, doesn't change the world long-term. Raising leaders does.

Dr. Robert E. Coleman's book *The Master Plan of Evangelism,* with Billy Graham's foreword, has become a worldwide classic with more than three million copies sold. I only met him in his late eighties—but still going strong—when he came to speak in Montreal in 2013. His counsel on the need to focus on the hard but strategic work of training those who will make disciples and lead—rather than focusing our energy on solving the felt needs of "the masses"—is so well-put, I couldn't have said it better:

> Yet in appraising the tragic condition of affairs today, we
> must not become frantic in trying to reverse the trend over-
> night. Perhaps that has been our problem. In our concern

to stem the tide, we have launched one crash program after another to reach the multitudes with the saving Word of God. But what we have failed to comprehend in our frustration is that the real problem is not with the masses—what they believe, how they are governed, whether they are fed a wholesome diet or not. All these things considered so vital are ultimately manipulated by others, and for this reason, before we can resolve the exploitation of the people we must get to those whom the people follow.

This, of course, puts a priority on winning and training those already in responsible positions of leadership. But if we can't begin at the top, then let us begin where we are and train a few of the lowly to become the great. And let us remember, too, that one does not have to have the prestige of the world to be greatly used in the Kingdom of God. Anyone who is willing to follow Christ can become a mighty influence on the world providing, of course, this person has the proper training.[186]

A NEO PROBLEM

As I sit in various global meetings of Christians, I sense a subtle unease among some about the rapidly changing global mission trends in the world. In some mission agencies, there has been clear tension between local/indigenous mission leaders in hitherto mission-receiving countries and their Western contemporaries because the former feel they have come of age and don't need this "neo-colonization." That may be arrogant; yet considering the degree of the historical paternalism among some, I'm not surprised at this knee-jerk reaction.

Tom Steffen, in commenting on one of the latest works of my friend and mentor Paul Borthwick (writer of the foreword to this book), is spot on: "Relevant roles still remain for North Americans, but new attitudes and strategies will be required. *Western Christians in Global Mission* offers intentional strategies to the humble so that a new era of missions can be discovered and learned together with genuine partners from the Majority World."

Whichever way you look at it, the business of changing the world has changed and so we have a *neo* problem. This is where the international student, again, steps in to save the day. I find the international student the sort of perfect emerging leader to bridge this gap. If he is given the solid attitudes, mindsets, and skillsets, while being educated in the things the West does best—yet he has the skin color and knowledge of language and culture to be able to fit in and be easily accepted by the people groups in his country of origin when he returns—he is the perfect hybrid the church and all creation are crying to see!

In this vein I think of Bakht Singh.

BAKHT SINGH

Bakht came to Canada as an international student from India. He was a Sikh from the Punjab region. Apparently his parents had resisted sending him to England for postgraduate studies because they feared he would be converted to Christianity. He eventually went to England and ironically fell for a life of partying.

Later, Bakht found himself studying agriculture at the University of Manitoba in Winnipeg, Manitoba, where the love of a simple couple, John and Edith Hayward, did something to him. With simple mealtime prayers and things like that, soon Bakht Singh became a believer and follower of Christ.

Bakht Singh returned to India and began a worldwide indigenous church-planting movement that saw more than 10,000 local churches planted before he passed away in the year 2000.[187] By the way, there were 250,000 people at his funeral!

Two couples among my ISMC staff, who both used to serve in India, testify of these things. In fact, both sets of couples were married by Bakht Singh.

EVEN MASTERCARD GETS IT...SORT OF

In a few gatherings where I've said this, I can be sure some church leaders were quite unhappy with me, but really, "is it not enough for Mastercard to take our money? Should they take our mission too?"

For a few years now, the Mastercard Foundation has instituted a "Scholars Program," a *$500 million, ten-year initiative through which the Foundation seeks to inspire young people—particularly from Africa—to lead change and make a positive social impact through education.*[188]

Partnering with McGill University, University of Toronto, and University of British Colombia in Canada (and others like Duke in the USA), Reeta Roy, president and CEO of the MasterCard Foundation, is confident "the MasterCard Foundation Scholars Program will develop next-generation leaders who will have a transformational impact in developing countries."[189]

UBC alone has a $25 million cut, and is expecting to welcome seventy-seven undergraduate and thirty-five Master's students over the next ten years.

While Mastercard is right in targeting leadership potential and using the process of schooling to engender change, I must say they haven't got the whole truth. Schooling and education are not the same, you see. You can be very schooled yet very uneducated.

Over the past one hundred years, Africa has had literally thousands trained as foreign students, but how much impact have we seen from them? I usually tease my Nigerian friends that you could even fill a whole stadium with just Nigerian PhDs, and so what? How is that really making a differ-ence in Africa's most populous nation?

I once cried to the Lord about this because it seemed a mystery to me. The answer I received was that developing nations invest in international stu-dents' education, yes, but it is almost entirely academic or technical knowl-edge (engineering, medicine, law, etc.). No one really teaches them hardcore leadership skills and competencies.

I sincerely believe that intentional, specific leadership training is the key to fully realizing how strategic reaching out to these international students from the developing world is. This is part of my mission. Unless we think outside the box in this way, simply churning out graduates and postgradu-ates without intentional leadership development won't get us any different results than we have had in the past century.

I have shared emerging leadership snippets from the past and present and from almost every continent so far. Let me not leave you without sharing two impact stories from Clement and Julie that touch on both Europe and Oceania...and oh, simultaneously scratch the Francophone world a bit.

LIGHT IN PARIS

When I met the Chinese-French student from Paris in Montreal, Clement Dang-Vu, there really was nothing extraordinary about his countenance—except this visible eagerness to learn all he could about leadership. Clement wasn't in town for the usual four years of undergraduate work; this was a few months' stint as part of his university program in France.

At the time, September 2010, I had been invited by the senior pastor of Montreal Chinese Alliance Grace Church (where I now pastor) to take the youth through some leadership training sessions from EQUIP's *Million Leaders Mandate*, Notebook One. Clement joined later—he missed the first session, comprising two lessons—but "chased" me until I did a one-on-one with him to catch up. I remember very well—in the basement library of the Peoples Church of Montreal.

See his email on 4 October, 2010 [unedited]:

— — — — — — — — — — — — — —

Hello Dr. Yaw,

I'm Clément from France and I asked you if I could have the documents concerning the leadership.

As I said to you, I would like to use what I have learned, thanks to you, in order to teach it to members of my church.

Indeed, I think that it is necessary to have a formation about leadership, vision, planning...things that miss in most of churches ...

I know that you're going to leave the country, so let's meet after your return for the two first lessons that I missed!

By the way, thanks for the preaching of today. This week, I had a course Tuesday about drinking water and I was really interested by this topic. I began to get some information, and I had a thought: work for a company of drinking water, so that I can go abroad and put some stuff so that people in Asia/Africa, can have drinking water. And during your preaching, when you spoke about the fact that every fifteen seconds, a child dies because of poor water, I was so moved. And I understood that it was certainly NOT a coincidence, that these thought moved me in the same week at two different places who seem to have

nothing to do with another. I mean course and preaching ...
it should have no link!! But it does ... not because of "fate."
However, because of God =) I'm so happy that he used
you to confirm a thought that started in my heart during
that course from Tuesday.

So let's keep contact, and I hope to see you soon!
Be blessed,
Clément

— — — — — — — — — — — — —

Clement was excited. We met, I taught and mentored. Fast-forward a
year later, Clement was back in France and wrote:

23 Sep 2011

Hello Doctor!
I'm ready for the presentation of the first leadership lesson!

Can you pray that people in my church may be touched
by the lesson and the Holy Spirit?

04 October 2011
Hello Dr. Yaw,

It went fine, I'll have the second lesson this Sunday! The
first lesson was nice, there were 15 people who were there
and motivated to hear much about it!

And now the 'leader' everyone sees (but have no clue how he became so):

12 January 2012
Hello Dr. Yaw!

I'm almost finished with the teaching of leadership equip! I've already done 5 lessons, so there is the strategic planning lesson remaining :)

I was the first time that I teach people, and I really love it. The pastor and the ancient [elders] of my church told me that I had the gift of teaching.

So after equip, I'll continue to do that.

Thanks again for this opportunity you gave to me, by sending me these documents freely and by teaching me!

In Paris, Equip begins to be taught but it's reserved for Pentecost people, so not may churches have this teaching.

I'll try to teach this in other moment!

I'm still in touch with Clement. And not too long ago, just about when I wanted to share part of his story with the Intervarsity USA staff in St. Louis, I emailed him about that. He sent me an update.

January 2014
So many time has passed since our last encountering!!

Well, I'm well. I'm gonna marry Tatiana a beautiful girl end of August 2014.

My ministry of evangelist goes well. I'm part of a formation for evangelist (the French declination of Leighton Ford evangelist ministry). It lasts 2 years and I'm at my last year. In my local church (suburbs of Paris), I'm deacon of evangelism and we could launch an evangelization week in October 2013. The last two years, I used almost my whole vacation to do evangelization camp. I really like to speak to people about the good news of Jésus-Christ died for repenting sinners. My church is still little (40 members in the French part and 40 members in the Chinese part). But I really like the fellowship communion and the fact that almost one third of the French group has understood the importance of the Great Commission. It's so endeavoring!!!

I speak about holidays because, well, I work for more than two years in water flood risk prevention. It's very interesting and I have good contacts with my colleagues. Last Christmas, I offered them, and even my boss lol, a Bible and a guide to read it every day. It's not always easy to work in the secular world but as for now, I know that my place is here.

With my network here in Paris, we launched a T4T group (inspired from the book Training for trainers, from Steve Smith and Ying Kai, you definitely have to read it!!!). The goal is to have a process in small groups where we learn about basics of disciple life to make other disciples (and not Christians who attend the church only the Sunday).

As a leader, I use a lot my smartphone to get meetings, events so it's looks like the chart you gave me.

If you have a question about me, don't hesitate. I'm eager to reply you a more developed answer.

By the way, I'm honored you name me in one of your speech. Could I have access to this speech?

And you? What are doing now? Are you full-time in ministry or do you work in the secular world?

Be very blessed and experiment the new life of Jesus every day.

What if I had just met Clement and only ate hot dogs with him? Easy ministry or strategic ministry?

NO JOB, NO HOUSE, NO DOG, NO KIDS, NO ORDINARY LIFE

"You yourselves are our letter, written on our hearts, known and read by everyone. You show that you are a letter from Christ, the result of our ministry, written not with ink but with the Spirit of the living God, not on tablets of stone but on tablets of human hearts."[190]

"Did I really have to commit to this Skype phone call before Julie's flight tonight?" I asked myself. I had met Julie just once, in Kamloops, when she was an international student from France at Thompson Rivers University. Through Dan (the then city director) and our amazing Kamloops team, Julie could testify that (and we have her full testimony in our custom-made New Testament Bibles from the Canadian Bible Society), *"if it was in France that I was spiritually born; then it is in Canada that I began to walk."*

The Lord used my visit in October 2013 to also bless and challenge her immensely, especially toward God-given purpose and leadership, and we have kept in touch since then. For example, she happily sent me an email when she was about to be baptized by Pastor Dan.

I really wanted to see her face (albeit via Skype), speak with her, and pray for her as she headed back home, yet I was still asking, *"Did I really have to commit to this Skype phone call before Julie's flight tonight?"* You see, I was running late (thanks to traffic!) on my drive from New York City to Washington, DC on Monday, May 19, 2014, yet I *knew* I had to pull over and call Julie and Preeti (the Indian president of our Kamloops FOCUS club who was with her).

I'm glad I did—for just twenty minutes. With Julie's permission, I would like to share the email she sent to me the day after (when she had arrived back home to France). Julie Pieters (and her letter) is a sample of the letters my staff, prayer partners, and financial supporters write every day, as together we *empower international students to impact the world through Jesus Christ.* I wanted to cry. While you enjoy her *unedited* written letter, remember that *she herself* is our letter! *This* is why we do what we do:

From: Julie PIETERS
Date: 20 May, 2014 8:28:16 AM EDT
To: Yaw Perbi
Subject: Bien arrivée en France !! =)

Dc Yaw,

I am in France now, completely jetlag, but safe. It is awesome to see my family, I realize now how much I missed them... =)

I was thinking of the prayer you made for me this morning, and of the passion for Christ burning in and through you. I want to tell you that you are an example for me. You know my story, you know that I didn't really know anything about Christ before coming to Canada, though He healed me with his mighty power. Dc Yaw, I can't recognize myself! Or rather, I don't know who the old Julie was. I completely changed! Now I have an identity. Now I have found the meaning of life, I have a purpose driven life! Dc Yaw, I can't even express with words how much I want to dedicate myself to Him, for His kingdom and His glory! Tears come in my eyes as I realize how much I love Him... Dc Yaw, I just want to lay down my life for Him, but even those words are not enough to express what I feel! I want him to use me every single minute of my life!! I pray that my mouth could never help itself from sharing his love and his words! I just want to shout it out, to tell the entire world!! I will work for Him as long as He lets me live! I am happy to see that I am 21, and by God's grace I have a lot of years before me to impact the world!

Dc Yaw, I don't want to get a job, a house, a dog, have 2 children and live an ordinary life. I am not saying anything against this type of life first because there are many different ways of doing ministry, and second because there is a time for everything. I am just saying that right now, I feel like a fire inside of me for Jesus and I can't just sit down and think about it. I need to go and shout it out!!! I don't know yet how God is going to use me, but I want to be an ambassador of His love and Word to the entire world! I am very excited to go to New Zealand and learn more about him!! Also I wonder what He has in store for me for after NZ. Because that I have no idea, and it is totally up to Him... I trust Him with all my heart. He will show me where He wants me to go after December. =) Life is so exciting when we know Jesus Dc Yaw, so exciting!!

Sometimes we just get too much into the things of this world, and we worry about different things, like when are we going to meet our husband/wife, and all these things, and we forget that He has a perfect mighty plan for us, and we don't have to worry about anything. I just pray that He will always have the priority over all these things, in my minds as well as in the reality.

Thank you so much again for caring so much for me, and Preeti and many others as you do. You are telling the world about Jesus, you are on every continent, you are busier than a businessman yet you take time to skype, email and pray for me. Thank you very much for that, I really value it. I will never forget the words you sent me in one of your first emails: "God doesn't called qualified people, He qualified those He calls." AMEENN!! =)

May God bless you abundantly and may He make a way for you to see your family more often. I pray that you will continue to impact people as you do. I pray for all those who have listened, are listening and will listen to you that God will open the eyes of their hearts and the Holy Spirit will fall upon them while you talk so they might see Jesus through you! May your gift of seeing new potential leaders be even more powerful so leaders of every nation will rise up and preach the Gospel to fulfill God's mighty plan!! Amen!

Julie Pieters

You bet I was encouraged to keep writing such "human letters." Was it easy ministry, pulling over from the highway to speak with Julie (not to mention following up on our relationship)? You bet not. But was it strategic? Absolutely!

I'm still in touch with Julie. In pursuing her apparent call, she was in New Zealand for six months, and then another six months, at a Capernwray school studying the Bible and being trained as a leader, a world changer.

Just before this book went to press I had the joy of visiting Clement in Paris and Julie in Lille. It was breathtaking just listening to them and watching them impact a "post-Christian France" right before my eyes, including the hungry and homeless on the streets. I'm still watching how all of this unfolds and impacts France, one of the most secular countries in the world yet with a 10% (and growing) Muslim population, and the world at large.

HIT OR MISS

The incredible potential impact of international students in and on leadership in their original countries cannot be overemphasized. Yet we haven't seen as much impact as we possibly could.

Quite honestly, with the tens of thousands of international students the developing world has sent all over the world to be trained, for example, one would expect much more impact from them than we've seen or are even currently experiencing.

I'm afraid that unless we are more strategic and intentional about raising godly, effectual national leaders among international students, including contextualizing our leadership lessons and properly preparing them for re-entry (with its reverse culture shock and all), what Adrian Hastings rather bluntly said of the first indigenous Ghanaians with leadership promise who were trained and ordained in Europe as ministers may be true in our times, too. Jacobus Capitein and Philip Quaque were prominent among these foreign students from Africa. Says Hastings:

> *"In missionary terms they were all failures...gifted individuals, blossoming in Europe but tied in Africa to a tiny white slaving community and only serving beyond it a rather nominally Christian fringe of mulattos living in the shadow of a fort."*[191]

THE SELECTION OF A LEADER

Perhaps the hardest part in this strategic ministry of raising leaders is where to start; and with whom to start. What is the way the Master went? *"One of those days Jesus went out to a mountainside to pray, and spent the night praying to God. When morning came, he called his disciples to him and chose twelve of them, whom he also designated apostles."*[192]

Need I say that this ought to be done *very* **prayerfully**? Someone once humorously quipped how Jesus spent the whole night praying before choosing His disciples, yet one of them was a thief and betrayer. Imagine if He hadn't prayed! Spiritual discernment beats any 'shopping list' of characteristics. You ask the prophet Samuel![193]

Apostle Paul points to the FAITHful to be selected.[194] Therefore prayerfully select among the many, the few people God lays on your heart who exhibit FAITH:

- Faithfulness (trustworthiness, integrity),

- Availability,

- Initiative and Influence (not necessarily in a huge way),

186

- **T**eachability (humility), and

- **H**unger (to learn and to change the world!).

If they were "already-made," then they wouldn't quite need you and me, right? But these are basic characteristics to look out for if all your hard, strategic work is likely to yield fruit. Jesus' Twelve were quite a rough bunch—diamonds in the rough. They were far from perfect, but exhibited a lot of FAITH—well, most of them, most of the time!

THE MAKING OF A LEADER

So you've finally prayerfully settled on your FAITHful young men and women. Now what? Whatever best practices and syllabi one decides to adopt and adapt, the following nine principal pillars must be present in order to intentionally and properly develop godly, effectual global emerging leaders (each one introduced by a verse from the life of the greatest leader who ever lived):

1. PROCESS—*"Come follow me and I will make you"*[195]

From start to finish one has to think "process"; even before selecting. Process, process, process! It cannot be a hit-and-run. A little (say an hour) every week for one year (better still, two to three years), will be much more beneficial than three days of cramming at some random once-every-three-years leadership conference. This is because, as one of my leadership mentors, John Maxwell says, *"Leadership is built daily; not in a day."*

In fact, in EQUIP circles we say, *real deep and lasting change doesn't take place in rows* [as in typical church/classroom/conference settings] *but in circles* [regular small group settings like Jesus' Twelve].

One would think the Savior of the world would come in big time to the masses and with one swipe and in a few seconds finish the job—a *microwave* oven approach. Yet He painstakingly and unhurriedly selects a few men to follow Him and *crockpot*-cook them, simmering, over three-and-a-half years. "As one might expect, these early efforts of soul winning had little or no immediate effect upon the religious life of his day, but that did not matter greatly."[196] We know that in the end these were the few *crockpot men* that turned the world upside down![197]

2. PROXIMATE—*"He appointed twelve that they might be with him"*[198]

Our students want relationship—don't we all? One's leadership development practice has to be relational. Celine's email revealed, "They are interested in meeting and becoming friends with the "native" [Canadian] but find it difficult to have conversation with them because of the language. They seem eager to mix with Canadians."

Friendship and a mentoring relationship is the best context for great leadership development. Life-on-life in real time. Actions do speak louder than words and *modeling* is a very powerful way of teaching. Jesus Christ was a master at this. For three-and-a-half years He poured His life into twelve men who ended up looking and acting like Him (long after He was gone) such that the authorities of the day actually, "took note that these men had been with Jesus."[199] No wonder—He selected and appointed them not first to work or go lead, but "that they might be *with* Him." (emphasis mine)

"When one stops to think of it," says Coleman, "this was an incredibly simple way of doing it. Jesus had no formal school, no seminaries, no outlined course of study, no periodic membership classes in which he enrolled his followers. None of these highly organized procedures considered so necessary today entered into his ministry. Amazing as it may seem, all Jesus did to teach these men his way was to draw them close to himself. He was his own school and curriculum."[200]

3. PRACTICE—*"He sent them two by two"*[201]

It's got to be more than "just hang out with me" and certainly not just another "book work"—it has to involve practical action. Remember the email about these students not wanting to study leadership because of their misconception of what leadership is? At least they didn't mind commenting about their preferred mode of learning, should they ever embark on a leadership development journey. Hear them (again from Celine's feedback):

> *"If they would study leadership, they would like to be active participants, in the form of a case study where they would interact with each other. They are less interested in a "lecture on leadership." They prefer a question where they would need to come together and "work out" an answer."*

A good way a lot of campus ministries offer practice is by giving students leadership **positions**. But without intentionality about the role, training for it and essential feedback, one may not get the desired results.

Short-term **projects** also very much help in training leaders. During ISMC's thirtieth anniversary in 2014, one such project called *Hike for Higher Education* in conjunction with Compassion Canada[202] was aimed at inculcating in emerging leaders a sense of giving back and fundraising skills.

Combining the *process* of being *proximate* (relationship and modeling) and *practical* will look like this: Watch me do it → I teach you to do it → I do it with you → I watch you do it → You go teach someone else, too.

4. PARADIGM-SHIFTING— *"You have heard it said...but I tell you"*[203]

"Ideas have consequences."[204] I'm afraid that the world view international students have will trump whatever technical knowledge they've gained to secure their college degree. *Any day!* No wonder people may be Ivy League-trained but still engage in dastardly cultural practices.

Said Paul Marshall, "[A]ny development program that fails to take into consideration the prevailing belief system of a people and the possible influence of this belief system on the proposed development plan runs a serious risk of foundering before it gets off the ground."[205]

Any leadership training should involve transformation *by the renewing of the mind*.[206] Beliefs, attitudes, and mindsets must be challenged and alternative paradigms introduced.

Of course Jesus knew that, and so several times He literally turned the minds of His disciples upside down. "You have heard it said," He would begin, and introduce the old paradigm ("stinkin' thinkin'," as Zig Ziglar would call it). And then the shift: "But I tell you!" In the Sermon on the Mount alone, He did a rapid fire paradigm-shifting on murder, adultery, oaths, revenge, and enemies.

The nations of the world are shaped by their paradigms, from African or Asian traditional worldviews to Communism. If we do not introduce our emerging leaders to a Biblical worldview, all our work is in vain, for "ideas have consequences."

5. PURPOSE-DRIVEN—*"As the Father has sent me, even so I am sending you."*[207]

International students ought to be taught that each of them was created by God for His five-fold purposes of: worship, fellowship, discipleship, service, and mission.

And by an assessment of their S-H-A-P-E,[208] be helped to discover the *specific* area(s) of calling where they were made by God to lead by serving.

Who else is going to teach them that "the place God calls you to is the place where your deep gladness and the world's deep hunger meet" (Federick Buechner) and which will bring God the highest glory?! It is sad when, after all their training and the exposure these students get, they just end up as victims of the infamous rat race and succumb to a life of materialism, 'just working a job' and the like. If we don't come alongside these young, impressionable minds and hearts and show them the way to a purposeful life, how else do we expect them to turn out?

I find that some ISM staff are overly concerned that many of these students don't physically return to their countries and go and make the impact they had hoped. But I insist, that is none of our business. Ours is to faithfully teach them how to discover God's specific purpose for their lives, including geographical location and line of work, and leave them and their God to flesh it out. Sometimes, geographically speaking, God's leading may neither be to their country of origin nor the one they studied in, but a third option. Just teach them "how to fish" for God's purpose.

6. PRINCIPLE-CENTERED—*"Verily, verily I say unto you..."*[209]

Often when Jesus was about to state a principle—a timeless, universal truth—he would begin thus: "Verily, verily I say unto you" or in modern English, "Truly, truly I say to you..."

The way the very contemporary version of the Bible known as *The Message* puts Jesus' Great Commission gives a refreshing view of it which really goes to underscore that discipleship has a lot to do with intentional *training and instruction*. It says, *"Go out and TRAIN everyone you meet, far and near, in this way of life, marking them by baptism in the threefold name: Father, Son, and Holy Spirit. Then INSTRUCT them in the practice of all I have commanded you..."*[210] (emphasis added)

Every game has rules; so does the game of life. So does leadership. Until people are trained in the principles of surgery, they won't make great surgeons. Until we train and instruct in the principles of servant leadership, how could we expect people to just turn out as worthy servant-leaders?

The principles taught must be deeply Scripture-rooted. Don't forget that Paul asserts that there are some "basic principles of this world" that others teach, that really are no principles at all because any true principle must be Scripture-rooted (even if you don't have a book, chapter, and verse added to it).

See to it that no one takes you captive through hollow and deceptive philos-
ophy, which depends on human tradition and the basic principles of this world
rather than on Christ.[211]

There is no better manual for leadership training than the Word of God:
Basic **I**nstructions **B**efore **L**eaving **E**arth (BIBLE). All that pertains to life
and godliness is found therein; when we meditate upon it and do what it
says, we are guaranteed prosperity,[212] which every leader wants for himself
and should so desire for the people he leads. God said so to Joshua—that
the key to a prosperous life and leadership was His Truth, His Word, His
Principles—and every Israelite leader (the king) was to have the law written,
memorized and lived by.

I find that there are many leadership training manuals that state "leadership principles" without referring to their Scriptural text (and I say again,
chapter and verse do not necessarily have to be printed in black and white).
But I always look for the Scriptural underpinnings; if I don't find a Scriptural
basis for that so-called principle that is being taught, I throw it out!

Fads, theories and philosophies of men come and go; even "heaven and
earth will pass away" but Jesus said "my Word will never pass away."[213] And
quite apart from the training materials themselves being Scripture-based,
every one of these nine pillars undergirding this training must be conducted
in a way that affirms Scripture.

7.   CHARACTER-BASED—"You are the salt of the earth"[214]

Charisma without character is a disaster waiting to happen. Invariably
it does. How many brilliant or skilled leaders don't we know who totally
flunked because of a fundamental flaw in character?

Our students must be taught to be like Christ in character. To be H.I.S.
people[215]:

a.   Leaders of **H**umility (nothing to lose)
b.   Leaders of **I**ntegrity (nothing to hide)

c. Leaders of Simplicity (nothing to prove).

The entire process of sanctification or discipleship is toward this end—the character of Christ: love, joy, peace, patience, kindness, goodness, faithfulness, gentleness, and self-control, a.k.a. the fruit of the Spirit.

The number one quality in a leader the world is looking for today is character, especially integrity. Did you know that among the topmost impediments to development in the world is corruption? "By one estimate," says the World Bank Group president, "$20 to $40 billion are stolen from developing countries each year."[216] While I can understand all the research, infrastructural, and governance approaches the World Bank and others take to stem this, the bottom line is that corruption comes from a heart of sin.

Will we build leaders who are worth their salt? As we mentor, can we not only tell but model to our emerging leaders from all over the world, especially the developing world, *You are the salt of the earth. But if the salt loses its saltiness, how can it be made salty again? It is no longer good for anything, except to be thrown out and trampled underfoot.*

8. HOLISTIC—*"And Jesus grew in wisdom and stature, and in favor with God and man."*[217]

Our training is not holistic unless it touches the physical (including financial), spiritual, social, mental, and emotional dimensions of life and leadership.

All three Hs—Head, Heart, Hands—must be touched on in the leadership training syllabus and process.

"Head stuff" (knowledge) must include things like vision, strategic thinking, and decision-making. "Hands stuff" (skills) will include strategic planning, people skills, and communication skills. When I say "Heart stuff," I mean character issues like humility, integrity, simplicity, and courage.

One of the major reasons why I'm on this warpath—calling the world of ISM to be strategic about intentional, holistic leadership development—is that a lot of the schooling our international students engage in is technical head stuff. Then a lot of the church's efforts at reaching them is geared toward the heart stuff. Somewhere in all this mix, the essential hands stuff for leading effectively falls through the cracks. As we think outside our existing paradigms and practice of ISM, this is a key area to include in our ISM worldview and toolbox.

There's nothing as embarrassing and frustrating as a good man (great character) who is a bad leader (no leadership skills). I have witnessed many, even to the level of national presidencies. Not good; not a pretty picture at all.

9. SPIRIT-EMPOWERED—*"You will receive power when the Holy Spirit comes on you"*[218]

I'm saddened to see many a leader trying to solve the world's problems without spiritual power! You can't! After a thorough three-and-a-half year *process* of intentional training of the Twelve that was most certainly *proximate* 24/7, full of *practical* roles and projects, one that had been *paradigm-shifting, purpose-driven, principle-centered, character-based* and *holistic,* Jesus still basically says, *"There's one more thing, guys, wait."*

Wait? What do you mean wait? Come on! We're *ready to rumble!* The best of human preparation and intentions can only take our global emerging leaders so far. Jesus knew that. Don't forget that after all this thorough training, they had run away when He was arrested. That whole saga had been triggered by one of His own mentees, Judas Iscariot; and the "head prefect" of the Twelve himself, Simon Peter, had verbally denied his Master thrice in one night! Jesus knew exactly what He meant when He said, *"wait in Jerusalem until you have received **power** from on high."*

In 2007, I was invited to join a handful of Lausanne leaders in a meeting in Budapest, Hungary, where there were a lot of discussions, especially idea generation and planning for Cape Town 2010. In these gatherings, as far as I've experienced, there is a subtle "Who's Who of Christianity" that goes on. We may not even like to admit it, but there's a bit of Christian elitism when it comes to those who have been to the Christian "Ivy Leagues" like Gordon-Conwell, Wheaton, Fuller, or Moody.

Anyway! At some point I remember saying to the group, *"Guys, no one went to a better Bible school than the disciples."* They were not just studying the Word, they *lived* with the Word *Himself;* the Word made flesh! They did not just *believe* that Jesus died and rose again—they were there, they saw and felt the danger of death—as a matter of fact, did they not all run away on the night He was arrested? They did not read a story, someone else's account; in fact, I love the way John the Beloved put it in his first epistle. He says, *"We proclaim to you the one who existed from the beginning, whom we have heard and seen. We saw him with our own eyes and touched him with our own hands. He is the Word of life."*[219]

So I continued my babbling, *"Yet* He told them *not* to go about preaching, teaching, leading, healing, whatever, *until* they had received the power of the Holy Spirit from on high."

It's true these trainees of ours may have encountered Jesus personally in the spiritual, it's true they may have been discipled and trained in leadership. Now they have the *authority/right* to be leaders in their contexts, communities, and countries, but they still don't have *power*! It's like laying out all the electrical wiring in a house one is building; but until the house is connected to the national grid and electricity kicks in, there's *no power*!

Jesus said *all* authority in heaven and on earth was His.[220] Consequently, He was, in turn, authorizing His followers (including us) to go and love and lead the world in His authority. "All the wiring is in place *but wait* in Jerusalem until you have received the *power* when the gift of the Holy Spirit comes on you, *and then* you will be my witnesses, my leaders globally." Authority is the *right* to do; *power* is the *ability* to do.

Even Jesus, fully God, yet fully man, had to be anointed: *"And you know that God **anointed** Jesus of Nazareth with the Holy Spirit and with power. **Then** Jesus went around doing good and healing all who were oppressed by the devil, for God was with him."*[221] (emphasis mine)

We need spiritually powerful leaders in our world today, especially in the face of such bold evil in our day, evil with impudence! We need "Super Men" to challenge the status quo and deal head-on with the spiritual forces of darkness that are on the rampage. The only way I know of which makes a man transform into "Super Man" is the anointing. To be anointed means to be host to the person, power and presence of the Holy Spirit, God Himself!

The only thing I'm aware of that the disciples ever came to Jesus, on their own initiative, to teach them to *do* was *to pray*! They must have observed that that was His source of leadership power. He had *modeled* it (remember our training must be relational): *"One day Jesus was praying in a certain place. When he finished, one of his disciples said to him, "Lord, teach us to pray, just as John taught his disciples."*[222]

Prayerless leadership is powerless leadership. We need to teach emerging global leaders how to pray! With the enormity of the task that lies ahead of them, woe betides them if we teach them everything but that.

These nine things are what we've been doing through The HuD Group[223] over the past decade in many countries, and now figuring out the best ways and means to incorporate these at ISMC and other ISMs the world over. I've been completely sold out to this cause of raising holistic, godly, effectual, emerging, global servant-leaders—there's no other way to change the world. *Bar none!*

BRIDGING THE DICHOTOMY

Having the privilege of living in both the Global North and Global South, I see a significant dichotomy in the general approaches of the two worlds to leadership development. The former tends to put more significant weight on skills and the latter on spirit. So I meet very well-organized and skillful Western leaders who can't even fast and pray, let alone cast out a demon. Then I meet tongues-speaking, prayer-warrior leaders from the developing world who don't even know what a strategic plan looks like! Both worlds need to *think outside the box* and marry skill *and* spirit.

ISMC H.E.L.P.S. TO H.E.A.L.

Our mission at ISMC is to *empower international students to impact the world through Jesus Christ*. This is the way I read it for practical purposes: ISMC H.E.L.P.S. international students to H.E.A.L. the world. So should you.

H.E.L.P.S. ➔ **H**ospitality and Friendship; **E**dification and Evangelism; **L**eadership development; **P**artnering; **S**ending

H.E.A.L. ➔ **H**ope; **E**dification and Evangelism; **A**ttitudinal change (paradigm shifts); **L**eadership

In my short spell with ISMs around the world, I see that most ministers' time and efforts are placed on the "H" and "E," what I'm calling "easy ministry" with little or no "L," "P," and "S" going on. Without the "H" and "E," no matter how strategic one wants to be, it will be a *hard* and frustrating ministry; in fact, no one will even show up. Yet without having the "L," "P," and "S" in mind and in the pipeline, ministry may be easy alright but will certainly not be strategic. May a new generation arise to think outside the box and do "easy, strategic ministry."

The "Friendship Funnel Strategy" in the illustration below summarizes well in a pictorial form how all of this "easy, strategic ministry" should flow. You may visit www.thinkingoutsidethewindow.org for further details and explanations.

If we will make the right deposit into these boxes (these special foreign students), oh, what precious gifts they will be to the places where God delivers them in His time, far and wide.

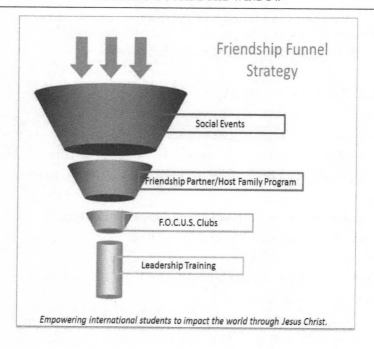

Friendship Funnel Strategy

Social Events

Friendship Partner/Host Family Program

F.O.C.U.S. Clubs

Leadership Training

Empowering international students to impact the world through Jesus Christ.

CURING KENYA

I just got off the phone with Isaac and shook my head in disbelief. I always knew he was going to make an impact—but you know that feeling you get when you expect something to happen, yet you still are surprised when it does?

The first time I met him and Emmanuel, they had come to look for me at my medical school residence in Accra. They knew of me through my books and seminars and were wondering if I could coach a bunch of them through what to expect during their impending medical school interview process. I gladly did.

But there was something about those two. Just the initiative they had taken alone made me see the flicker of leadership light. I loved them and mentored them. Through The HuD Group we put in all the above nine ingredients I believe should go into strategically preparing the next generation of mission and marketplace leaders.

When Isaac graduated from the University of Ghana Medical School after many achievements, including serving as president of the Christian Medical Fellowship (a position I held in my heydays, too!), I was so proud of him when he became an international student. I thought a global perspective of things would help greatly in his total formation. He was not just good enough for Ghana—he was good enough for the world. Having the hard choice between Harvard and Johns Hopkins, he chose the latter to pursue his Master's in Public Health.

In May 2014, I moved heaven and earth to ensure I was at his graduation in the *charming city* of Baltimore. I'm glad I could make it. Though the more formal stage of instruction in leadership and entrepreneurship passed long ago, the mentoring relationship and friendship goes on...unstructured...and only from time to time. One such time is when I checked on him and hung up shaking my head in disbelief. Though now an assistant faculty member at Johns Hopkins, he, for a few weeks, had to leave his dear wife in Baltimore and was en route to Kenya. Why?

These were his own words: "Dr. Pee [as many of my mentees affectionately call me], your boy is now a consultant to the Kenyan government's Ministry of Health." The young man I had the privilege of shaping in a small way, is now literally shaping the future of another country in a big way.

I'm still shaking my head. I rest my case.

COLEMAN'S CONCLUSION

Remember Dr. Robert E. Coleman's earlier counsel? How about his conclusion regarding the question of easy ministry or strategic ministry?

> Here is where we must begin just like Jesus. It will be slow,
> tedious, painful, and probably unnoticed by people at first,

but the end result will be glorious, even if we don't live to see it. Seen this way, though, it becomes a big decision in the ministry. We must decide where we want our ministry to count—in the momentary applause of popular recognition or in the reproduction of our lives in a few chosen who will carry on our work after we have gone. Really it is a question of which generation we are living for.[224]

Are we going to do the work of mission ourselves (deceiving ourselves that we could ever finish it on our own) or going to empower a myriad of others to? Are we going to just "spend" time with these international students, or will we "invest" time and other resources in them?

So choose this day *how* you will serve: easy ministry or strategic ministry? I must confess that many live and minister to international students with the mindset of this anonymous quote that deeply pierced my heart when I read it from Richard Stearns' book, *The Hole in our Gospel*: "*We have shrunk Jesus to the size where he can save our soul but now don't believe he can change the world.*" Let's make world-changers through Jesus Christ!

Now, even if we succeed in *thinking outside the window* of easy ministry, the next question will be, "so who's going to pay for all this?"

"*We have shrunk Jesus to the size where he can save our soul but now don't believe he can change the world.*"
~THE HOLE IN OUR GOSPEL

~13~

THERE GOES MY INDEPENDENCE!

Out the window! You mean I'm going to ASK for money?

"The three-and-a-half hour flight from Los Angeles to Minneapolis crept slowly. Every minute seemed to produce a new anxiety. I was going home to ask people to support my new ministry financially.
As we were about to land, I wiped the sweat from my clammy palm. The man across the aisle from me was reading "Death of a Salesman." How appropriate," I thought. I felt like a salesman. And I thought I was going to die."[225]
~BONNIE C. BISHOP

Money and mission are Siamese twins; I therefore find it very amusing that some "serious" missionaries don't want to have anything to do with it. Like someone humorously quipped, "The Gospel may be free but it takes money to send it." "And how are they to preach unless they are sent?"[226] And how are they to be sent without funds?

Coming from a continent that, for centuries, has mainly been a missionary-receiving one, I had *no idea* the extent to which individual missionaries from the West had to go to raise financial support from churches, family, friends, and business people in order to be able to embark on those "deadly voyages" to reach us. Thank you! Thank you! Thank you!

Some of us thought these "white people" were just well off and so could afford to give of some extra time and money for charitable work. Now I know better. Perhaps, those sent solely by local churches and denominations who fully financially supported their missionaries had it a bit easier on the financial side, but for the majority sent from mission agencies ("para-church"—by the way, I can't stand that term) they went (and still do) from home to home, church to church, business to business, organization to organization *raising their own support,* so-to-speak (I shall soon briefly comment on the flaw in that italicized phrase).

Now that it is our turn as the Global South to also "go," our eyes have been opened to this tremendous enterprise of raising funds for the mission. We have to do some serious *outside the box* thinking. This has not been in the thinking framework of many of us—and for the majority, the missionaries who came to bless them with the Gospel showed them their *works* but not their *ways.* In other words, they did not teach many of the folks in Africa, Asia, and Latin America how to raise resources for the mission. We were just to freely receive—and in the meantime—we were happy to.

But now the hour has come; we find ourselves on the *other* side and many are ill-equipped for the task. While we learn the best from the West, the tricks of the trade, the ropes, best practices, call it what you may, ultimately *we lift up our eyes to the hills. From where does our help come? Our help comes from the LORD, who made heaven and earth.* [227] As a colleague-preacher from Africa put it rightly, our help comes from *above; not abroad.*

FROM DEEP DOWN MY HEART TO YOURS

I've always wanted to make money—loads of it. And why not? Don't they say *money makes the world go round?* I started learning about money early.

I made a vow a long time ago—and challenged my medical school cohort too—that "I shall never be a poor doctor!" (sounds like an oxymoron, but it happens. A lot.)

This chapter has been the most difficult to write—I surmise it's because I'm still in the process of being *transformed by the renewing of my mind.*[228]

I still share this largely embarrassing chapter because I want you to know that I am also being stretched by the Lord in this area of money and missions, to *think outside the window.*

I want to particularly dedicate it to the new emerging generation of missionaries from the Global South. This money business in missions is all new to the majority of us, totally out of our thinking box, and if they could learn a thing or two from my successes and failures they could have a significant head start.

NO HELP! I WANT TO MAKE MY OWN MONEY

I set out in my early twenties to become financially independent. Don't forget, I'm the guy who wrote the three-book "Financial Whizzdom" series. Many acknowledge me as the "grandfather" of investment clubs in Ghana, having founded the premier investment club in the country, Medics Investment Club, while still a medical student. To date, my book, *Financial Whizzdom through Investment Clubs,* is still the only one in the country which comprehensively addresses the subject and has inspired the birth of numerous investment clubs nationwide.

My colleagues in the medical fraternity and I even co-founded a collective investment fund for (para)medics known as Mutual Medics (M²). Up till today, my good friend Elsie Awadzi (nee Addo), who now works for the International Monetary Fund in Washington, DC, keeps telling the story of how strange it was to find a medical student sitting in her Ghana Stock Exchange classes. Weirder still, one who knew more about business and investment than many from business school in the class!

I hold certificates from the Ghana Stock Exchange and Investment Funds Institute of Canada and have both investment and insurance licenses in the province of Quebec and Ontario respectively. For two-and-a-half years I consulted for Investors Group, Canada. Prior to that I had been with World Financial Group for about a year in Montreal and attended three of their scintillating business conventions in Las Vegas with my family in 2010, 2011, and 2012.

Anyele and I built a couple of businesses in Ghana; one of them, NEOparadigms Ltd., was mainly into corporate leadership training, consulting, and motivational media. I used to be so tickled by how half an hour of corporate training would often fetch me the equivalent of 25 percent of my monthly salary as a doctor!

A subsidiary bookshop called NEOwarehouse, was situated at a very busy intersection in prime Accra. It had provided employment for a few young people. We closed it down just before our exodus to Côte d'Ivoire (me in June, 2008) and Canada (Anyele in July 2008) respectively.

Since moving to Canada we've tried our hands at many business ventures. None of them really full-time, except financial consulting for two to three years. In early 2013 we decided to fully take advantage of all our John Maxwell following and reading over the years, investing nearly $10,000 for me to become an official John Maxwell Certified speaker, trainer, and coach. Suffice it to say, not only has it been a rewarding growth experience for me and my clients, we have made back that money and more.

Needless to say, we've always been quite entrepreneurial; we are entrepreneurs at heart.

SECRET FEAR

It was not until recently that the Lord revealed to me that the reason for my hyperactivity in the realm of finance, business, and investment is because I've always harbored a deep secret fear of being poor and unable to fend for myself, my family, and my purpose. And worse, I have such deep pride I want to be *independent* of everybody, including my parents.

Come to think of it, in the very origins of The HuD Group we largely determined (both spoken and unspoken) that we will not really ask for money. We did a few times, but the major way we funded our work across Ghana then (and later other places in West Africa) was through selling books I had authored. For over ten years now I have taken no royalties on the books. Now that I have a wife and children to look after, I've asked that that tradition be seriously reviewed!

When the Lord moved us to Canada, I had just resigned from medical practice (as soon as I returned to Ghana from Côte d'Ivoire) and knew I was solely coming to Canada as a missionary. From my "death day" in Côte d'Ivoire that had been my resolve—to spend the rest of my life preaching the Gospel and raising younger leaders.

So here I was in Montreal, a freelance minister of the Gospel mainly engaged in itinerant preaching and holistic leadership development both in Canada and internationally. No regular job; no regular income. Only "a prophet's reward" from speaking here and there and selling a few books (not royalties; actual difference between cost price and selling price).

Initially, Anyele's pay from being a research assistant and teaching assistant while the PhD track was still alive kept us barely going. We spent a considerable amount of time and money in the first few years dabbling in all kinds of business ventures; most of them network marketing companies proffering anything from insurance to weight loss potions.

We learned long ago that the path to substantial wealth creation that could significantly move the Kingdom of God forward was not a job; it was business and investment (the "B" and "I" quadrants, as Robert Kiyosaki would call it in his *Rich Dad Poor Dad* book series).

But beyond what we wanted, what was the even greater motivation was what we did *not* want: poverty (and all it comes with, especially dependence).

SEEK YE FIRST

We thought with this "good motive" and laudable end in mind—not to be poor but to make loads of money so we could finance God's work—the Lord would grant quick and easy success. We purchased our first investment property in Ghana while still living in a two-bedroom apartment in Montreal and were not doing badly, but not great...yet!

I remember once being asked by the first client who transferred over $200,000 worth of assets for me to manage when I was at IG: "Why do you want to be rich?" I proceeded to "lecture" this Christian elderly lady on all these amazing Kingdom goals I had!

I must admit that at some point the bent on getting financially independent was eating at the very thing for whose sake we thought we wanted to make money: ministry! The lines were beginning to blur between seeking *first* God's Kingdom (and He adding all these other things) and seeking these other things, money in particular, in the name of seeking God's Kingdom first.

We were intent on getting "financially independent" by 2012. In fact, in 2012 we liquidated almost all our shares on the Ghana Stock Exchange and invested $17,000 in some Tigrent real estate courses in Canada. An investor advanced us $50,000 and we set up a three-tier real estate company in Quebec. We had put offers on two multi-unit investment properties in two different cities in two different provinces (with some more in the pipeline) and had done our math: we were set to get "financially independent" by the end of 2012. *Seriously!*

One by one the Lord, in His providence, shut down deal after deal (trust me, it didn't feel so good then and we surely weren't smiling!). We are grateful that at least He preserved and favored our deal on our own family five-bedroom home in Pierrefonds, on the west island of Montreal. We were glad we finally had a "mission house" to host the people of God. Around this same time I was struggling with accepting the position of president of ISMC.

My paradigm and plan was that by thirty-five I would become a financially independent CEO. I could never have imagined that rather, by thirty-five, though I would become one of the youngest CEOs in Canada alright, I would not only be far from being financially independent; I would actually be *asking* people for money!

FIVE PARADIGM-SHIFTS THAT BLEW ME OUT OF MY WINDOW!

Becoming a missionary was hard enough; but asking me to "raise my own support" in addition was a bit much! Being a businessman and a missionary both require faith, loads of it. Faith that your vision will materialize, the mission will succeed, or that the 'product' will be loved and bought.

Part of that faith-life is being comfortable with not having a steady paycheck. I can remember many months in business when the business was actually eating me up, instead of feeding me! In fact, as my wife and I look back, we see so many parallels between business and missions, it is no wonder God used (and still does) the former as a training ground for the latter. I guess He did the same with Jesus (carpentry) and every one of His disciples. Interestingly, all of them were marketplace-trained; not seminary graduates from "the school of the Sadducees" or "parish of the Pharisees."

But while many entrepreneurs speak of "financial independence," the missionary has no such mindset or lingua. That was my first, painful paradigm shift.

PARADIGM SHIFT #1: INTERDEPENDENCE

Bryan Hehr blogs this well: "Most people dread sending out support letters and asking for money. I know quite a few who would rather get an extra job and give up their social life for six months to raise the money instead of allowing others to partner with them. I have been there as well."[229] Of course! Who wants to beg or look like one who does... or be thought of as one! Especially a medical doctor of my caliber!

I have been a motivational speaker for nearly two decades. I'm all for people being responsible and proactive. But we cross the line when we begin to feel like we don't need anybody else. Some even want to be independent of God!

As for independence from God, the lure of our first parents, Adam and Eve, that has never been an option for me. But surely what could be so wrong with independence from people?

The following words from Betty Barnett's classic, *Friend Raising*, penetrated straight into my heart and blew me out of my narrow, even toxic, "independence" mindset: "The call to a faith-support lifestyle is a call to interdependence. In today's culture this is revolutionary."[230] Revolutionary—thinking outside the window, indeed.

Betty hits the nail right on the head again: "Interdependence is not Christian welfare. It is the joining of forces to defend the faith and to fight the good fight."[231] The relationship between me and one of the friends I made in Montreal who supports our missionary endeavor, a high-ranking diplomat, illustrates this interdependence so well. He knows he can count on me for counsel, support, and prayer on sensitive issues and in high pressure times. Though he is an ambassador, when it comes to spiritual things, he looks to me for leadership. In turn, his diplomatic dollars do our ministry a lot of good. I cherish his friendship in life as profoundly as he respects my calling to ministry.

Yet, this interdependence is not an exact exchange.

PARADIGM SHIFT #2: UNEQUAL EXCHANGE

It has been a *huge* thinking outside the box for me, coming from the world of business where money is earned by *equivalent* exchange of goods and services, to the world of charity and missions where there is exchange alright (interdependence), but not quite in the same way.

Business essentially thrives on buying and selling while Kingdom finances are primarily based on giving and receiving.[232] If I have to allocate only an hour a week to visit with His Excellency (my friend the ambassador I just alluded to) because that's how much his monthly giving comes to at my "hourly rate" then there's a problem! A *big* problem.

Madam Barnett's YWAM co-worker, Earl Pitts, explains this well: "... in buying and selling we keep our resources to ourselves, and exchange with reciprocity, a measured transaction of equal value. We all engage in buying and selling—there's a time for buying and selling, and a time for giving and receiving. We need to have integration. Each fulfills important purposes. We pay rent and house payments; we buy clothes and groceries. It's part of life, but buying and selling is not to be the consuming mode of money transactions, especially among Christians."[233]

When the Lord called me from medicine into missions, I knew it was a higher calling, but I never perceived that it would also be a translation from the lower principle of "buying and selling" to a higher law of "giving and receiving." For as Barnett poignantly puts it, "One does not cancel out the other, but supersedes or transcends it... Giving and receiving is not canceled out by buying and selling. It is a periodic event which goes far beyond the ordinary."[234]

Now I'm really thinking outside the window, since *"giving and receiving (interdependence) is counter-cultural. It confronts and breaks the world's system of independence.... When buying and selling consumes us and becomes the priority of our life, we've lost the sense of how God wants to knit us together. We've fallen into the sin of the "love of money." We've lost the richness of giving and receiving."*[235] Worse still, "Satan would lure us into independence by the exclusive system of buying and selling. He is fully aware of the spiritual riches which will be released as we give and receive."[236]

It seems to me no words can more profoundly express the gross shortfall of a life of mere "buying and selling"/equal exchange like Jesus' question: "What can anyone give in exchange for their soul?"[237] If the Kingdom of God did not operate on such unequal transactions, how much would I have had to pay for my salvation in Jesus? This is another example to consider.

And so here I sit under deep conviction: "The precious things which have been given to us often hold far more value than those things we have purchased. Satan robs us often as we sit by, unaware. We must pursue God's ways of interdependence through giving and receiving, rather than the worldly virtues of brash independence. When we use the world's ways, we will have the world's brokenness...when we use God's ways, we will have His healing wholeness."[238]

I did not know how to receive before I became a missionary. In fact, I remember when I called a friend in Seattle, who used to work for Bill Gates at Microsoft, I was prayerfully gearing up myself for some tough questions. Why would I be asking him for money to be paid as a missionary? Rather than ask me that, it seems the Lord had been preparing his heart. He said something which I would never forget—it was meant to be an encouragement, I guess, but it still cut me somewhat: "Knowing you, I'm sure you would rather be on the other side [doing the giving; not the asking]." I am finally allowing the grace to receive to permeate my life.

PARADIGM SHIFT #3: ASKING IS NOT BEGGING

In many ways I consider myself as a transnational, bridging the worlds of Ghana and Canada. There are some years where I'm literally in my motherland every other month, although I'm a permanent resident of Canada.

On one such visit, I challenged the national director of a leading mission agency in Ghana on why his missionaries have not adopted the paradigm of raising support. He had tried to implement a partial support-raising scheme and had been met with a lot of resistance, not only because this fifty-year-old organization had not been bequeathed that tradition, but for two reasons, both of which will be addressed in this paradigm shift and the next.

At the time the national director and I were speaking, it was way into December and the staff had not yet been paid for the previous month. There was no money to pay. Yet, his staff wouldn't raise support because, "they didn't want to go abegging."

Of course, why wouldn't one feel like a beggar asking for money, albeit for God's work, when the prevalent worldview, sadly even among many Christians, is, "I earned this. I'm going to keep it!" Earn your own.[239]

I highly recommended a book that had totally shifted my own hitherto beggar paradigms to him, Henri Nouwen's *The Spirituality of Fundraising*. I encouraged him that I, too, had had to repent and be converted: "Fundraising is precisely the opposite of begging. When we seek to raise funds we are not saying, 'Please, could you help us out because lately it's been hard.' Rather, we are declaring, 'We have a vision that is amazing and exciting. We are inviting you to invest yourself through the resources that God has given you—your energy, your prayers, and your money—in this work to which God has called us.' Our invitation is clear and confident..."[240]

Contrast this with "I'm a beggar. I want a regular paycheck like normal people. I don't want donations that make me feel like I owe people."[241]

Nouwen remarks that even in business, marketing, and sales especially, "Those who are involved in big business know that you never get much money if you beg for it."[242]

The renowned author then speaks so fondly of a fundraiser who flat-out said, "I ask for money standing up, not bowing down, because I believe in what I am about. I believe that I have something important to offer." Without apology he invites people to be part of his vision.[243]

Now, I'm thinking outside the window.

PARADIGM SHIFT #4: DUH! IT'S PART OF THE MINISTRY!

The other roadblock, or rather mind block, the African missionaries were having, and which they even wanted to "guilt-trip" their boss with was: "if we should go spending our time raising money, when would we find time to do the *actual* work?" I relaxed in my seat and smiled when I heard that. I smiled because not only did I formerly think inside that same box, but I had observed that as many of my ISMC staff who thought that way never had enough money in their ministry accounts for the "real work."

I have been converted to the extent that I do not just "endure" raising money to move on to the "real work" of raising emerging leaders or sharing the salvation message or whatever. I actually *enjoy* doing this because it is an essential and *equally spiritual* part of everything else I do as a missionary.

In her very gracious preface to the 2004-released book of Henri Nouwen cited above, Sue Mosteller didn't hide the fact that, "Like many of us, Henri's vision began with the notion of fundraising "as a necessary but unpleasant activity to support spiritual things." But his passion for ministry and for living from a spiritual motivation led him further and deeper until he could finally say with conviction, "Fundraising is first and foremost a form of ministry.""[244]

I was glad to know that I was part of an "elite" group of repented and reformed ministers and missionaries who now shared Nouwen's conviction that, "Fundraising is as spiritual as giving a sermon, entering a time of prayer, visiting the sick, or feeding the hungry!"[245]

One such way I have come to appreciate the parallels between my sermons at the Chinese church almost every Sunday and traveling the world speaking for ISMC is this:

> As ministry, fundraising includes proclamation and invitation as well as conversion. "Fundraising is proclaiming what we believe in such a way that we offer other people an opportunity to participate with us in our vision and

mission." For Henri, the proclamation and invitation involve a challenging call to conversion for fundraisers and donors alike. "Fundraising is always a call to conversion." All are called into a new, more spiritual relationship with their needs and their resources. Henri encourages fundraisers to become more confident and joyful, standing up in their asking without apology. And in this vision they do not profit alone, because donors also participate in a new communion with others while becoming part of a much larger spiritual vision and fruitfulness.[246]

PARADIGM SHIFT #5: REAL PARTNERSHIP

Even before reading all this cool stuff about *Friend Raising* from Betty Barnett, I had learned some invaluable lessons about the importance of "raising more than money" from Doug Carter, the same EQUIP servant of God I mentioned in my prologue.

Doug is an amazing person in general, very warm and deeply caring every time I've met him, whether in my own niche in Canada or in his own back yard in the United States. But when it comes to fund development (fundraising) in particular, I've met very few who match his caliber. No wonder when my mentor John Maxwell and his brother Larry initially founded EQUIP in 1996 to train Great Commission leaders, it was Doug they settled on as their first employee.

I learned from Doug not to think *I am* the one doing the ministry and deserving of support from those who have the money to give. No! I have even had to gently rebuke some of those who support our ministry who put me on a higher pedestal and say, "*You* are the one who is doing something which makes your life count. We just make money."

No! No! No! **We are equal partners in this.** Like my friend Todd Ahrend, founder of the Traveling Team would say, when it comes to the Great Commission every Christian must either "send or go!" (or both).

I was glad to find out when I joined ISMC that they had long ago thrown out terms like "donor" and were using "partner." In fact, you will hardly hear someone talking about doing "fundraising;" we speak of "partner development."

John says this of the EQUIP Senior Vice President, "Doug not only knows how to raise needed funds, but he truly cares about the donors. He always endeavors to serve them, and he looks for ways to add value to their lives."[247] That's what I seek to do, too; not just milk corpulent Christian cash cows.

As equal partners, Doug has taught me to L.O.V.E. my partners, L.E.A.D. them, L.I.N.K. them and L.I.F.T. them.[248]

Again, "Doug's vocation in the realm of development has focused more on teaching givers to reflect the giving nature of Christ than about raising money."[249] So I pray for myself in this new *thinking outside the window* venture.

~~~

On a direct transatlantic flight from JFK, New York, to Accra I noticed one of my younger medical colleagues on board. I was so ecstatic to see him that I tried to hug his huge figure. I learned that his new wife was also somewhere on board the plane. At the time, this was my only fellow-doctor in the United States who was supporting our ISMC mission.

But the excitement of seeing him soon wore off with the realization that they weren't going to Ghana on a happy note. His wife had just lost her dad. When I found out the details, I resolved in my heart to modify whatever plans I had slated for Ghana and ensure I was able to go and "mourn with those who mourn."

Thank God I was able to. He was profoundly touched that I came—knowing how incredibly busy I can be, especially when I have a few days to do a whole lot before heading back to the other side of the Atlantic. Why did I? Because we are *truly* partners, sons of the same Father, whose vineyard we till *together*.

~~~

I listen to my partners because I value them, I open my heart to them and generously give in prayer, encouragement, and even physical gifts. I have learned to involve many of them; not just have a "watch me do it" kind of attitude. As equal partners, I don't take them for granted and that is why I thank them often and keep them informed and also try to facilitate their dreams.

Every reward that is mine because I preach the Gospel, win souls, and disciple leaders, I believe my doctor-friend (and all my partners) have an equal share in, for, "If you receive a prophet as one who speaks for God, you will be given the same reward as a prophet."[250]

Again, one other reason I so much love the term "partner development" is that it encourages my staff and I to go out there and *discover* those partners whom *God has already prepared* to join hands with us to work the field of souls. *Whenever God gives a* vision, *He would have already made the provision*. No, we don't go out there to "raise our own support." That's a faulty mindset; after all, "Who serves as a soldier at his own expense?"[251]

JESUS WAS THE FINAL NAIL

All of these paradigm shifts have been good, but you know what really nailed it for me? I was shocked and pleased synchronously to find that my Master, the one who called and chose me, saved and commissioned me, and after whom I pattern my life, Himself, who owns all the riches in the world, *chose to have His ministry financially supported by human partners,* especially women, like Magdalene, Joanna, and Susanna!

> *After this, Jesus traveled about from one town and village to another, proclaiming the good news of the kingdom of God. The Twelve were with him, and also some women who had been cured of evil spirits and diseases: Mary (called Magdalene) from whom seven demons had come out; Joanna the wife of Chuza, the manager of Herod's household; Susanna; and many others. These women were **helping to support them out of their own means.**[252] (emphasis mine)*

That has done it for me. Enough said!

IT'S NOT CALLED "FAITH MISSION" FOR NOTHING

So I now think outside my original windows—I am converted. I have repented of my unbelief, non-biblical, non-spiritual ways of thinking about raising finances and have turned to faith, trusting in God's will and way regarding missionary support.

One day God asked me, "What if I never made you wealthy?" That was a hard question. "What if, like Paul, I made *not ever having more than enough* a 'thorn in your flesh'?" I accepted that possibility.

The bottom line of this calling of ours is *faith*. Faith on my part and that of all my ministry partners and supporters in cash, moral support, and prayer.

I like the way Bryan Hehr summarizes how this faith exercise plays out on both sides of the fence.

> *For me it requires faith in these areas:*
> — *That God is calling me to go*
> — *and if He is, then He is the one who provides*

216

- *That my supporters trust in me and the work that I am doing*
- *That God is working through my partners in this process as well.*

For my partners:
- *They have to trust God will provide for them as they give their money away*
- *They have to trust in me and the work God is calling me to*
- *They have to trust God in the way He will bless them in this process (oftentimes not in the form of material blessing).*[253]

BUT HOW ABOUT "THE GENIUS OF THE '*AND*'"?

"The test of a first-rate intelligence is the ability to hold two opposed ideas in the mind at the same time, and still retain the ability to function."
(F. Scott Fitzgerald)

Having been through all of that and said all of that, however, I still want to challenge the way missions funding has been seen and done in the last two hundred years of the missionary enterprise. A little. It is true, individual missionaries have enlisted friends, family, church, and business people to support them in their mission, but the question is, must that still be the model, going forward into the next phase of global missions in the twenty-first century?

According to F. Scott Fitzerald's words above, it will take some significant thinking outside the window to be able to "hold two opposed ideas in the mind at the same time:" the two apparently opposed ideas of "buying and selling" versus "giving and receiving" in funding the 21st Century missionary enterprise.

Jim Collins, author of the best-seller *Good to Great,* challenges us about "the tyranny of the '*or*'" (which dictates that one must choose from two seemingly contradictory paradigms) as against "the genius of the '*and*'" (the possibility of holding both in balance).

For the past few years I have become a great fan and consumer of Bill Hybels' annual Global Leadership Summit. During the break at one of the summits I picked up an old CD recording of an interview he conducted with Jim Collins years before in which the best-selling author and lecturer did a great job of summarizing what he meant by the terms above.

According to Dr. Collins, we live in a world where we are brutally battered by *the tyranny of the 'or'*; which basically says we always have to make choices between "A" *or* "B", short-term *or* long-term, serving a higher purpose *or* making profits, having self-management *or* discipline, high productivity *or* high quality, etc. (a variety of all kinds of *"or"* that hit us.)

However, *the genius of the 'and'* (which is a rejection of *the tyranny of the 'or'*) is that we're going to figure out the great task of how to do "A" *and* "B", short-term *and* long-term, serving a higher purpose *and* making money, having self-management *and* discipline, etc. That we're going to put all these ends together that *seem contradictory* and make them work together.

So I dare ask: Must it be *the tyranny of* either "buying and selling" *or* "giving and receiving" in supporting missions and missionaries, or could the Lord be calling a new generation to *the genius of the 'and,'* "both and"?

I recently met two Caucasian businessmen after speaking at the Christian Business Men's Committee in Winnipeg, Manitoba, who have set up a profit-making enterprise solely for the purpose of funding reconstructive surgery for rape victims in the Democratic Republic of Congo. I'm not speaking of "social entrepreneurship" per se. I don't know if this hybrid I perceive even has a name.

The only way to finish the task of the Great Commission is to think outside the window, outside the box. Could we not combine *buying and selling* with *giving and receiving* like owning international student hostels which return good money to missions and yet are themselves ministry? Must it be either/or?

"One term being used for this new mission movement is "business as mission." Business in and of itself is the ministry and instrument of mission.

It is about releasing the entrepreneurs and business professionals within the church in order to transform the world through their business activities."[254]

Again, could we not have *both* traditional missionaries (those who have to go through my kind of conversion above to raise financial support for their mission) *and* many more "tentmakers" in finishing the task? Tentmakers are "believers in all people groups who have a secular identity and who, in response to God's call, proclaim Christ cross-culturally [which we now do in every major world city anyway, even in the West, because the world has come to our doorsteps!]. Tentmakers witness with their whole lives and their jobs are integral to their work for the Kingdom of God."[255]

In fact, when I became ISMC president, we had approximately eighty staff, half being "Career Staff" or traditional missionaries and the rest "tentmakers" we call "Associate Staff" (not counting the 500 *amazing* volunteers from coast to coast). At the time of writing we had catapulted to about 110 staff, with about 85 percent of the new staff being tentmakers. There is no way God's "big, hairy, audacious" vision for us to double our impact by doubling our number of staff and ministry cities in two years could be attained by looking only to bring on traditional missionaries.

Although many trace the two hundred-year history of modern missions largely to William Carey and his generation, and see him as a true traditional missionary role model, what many don't realize (even I didn't until recently) is that even Carey went to India as a shoemaker. He said, "My business is to witness for Christ. I make shoes to pay my expenses." William Carey was neither a professional theologian nor a pastor, but a tradesman who loved to do mission work for Christ.

It seems to me that, while perceiving the future of missions funding to be very dependent on thinking outside the traditional box, not even Carey was that traditional, for two hundred years ago he said, "We have ever held it to be an essential principle in the conduct of missions, that whenever it is practicable, missionaries should support themselves in whole or in part through their own exertion."[256] It seems quite ironic to me that we may need to go back two hundred years to think outside the window again.

THE BROADER CALL TO THINK OUTSIDE THE WINDOW

If *thinking outside the window* includes new ways of processing life and mission like *the genius of the 'and'* paradigm, then 21st Century mission is:

- Not either hospitality *or* evangelism but *both* in *"friendship evangelism"*
- Not discipleship *or* evangelism but *discipleship onto conversion*
- Not either discipleship *or* leadership but *discipleship into leadership*
- Not easy *or* strategic ministry but *simple, strategic ministry*
- Not "full-time career missionary" *or* "associate tent-making staff" but "both and"
- Not local missions *or* global missions but *thinking globally and starting locally*; and
- Not either "giving and receiving" *or* "buying and selling" but "both and."

Even mission money from the West *and* the Global South.

~14~

MONEY FROM AFRICA?

Now, that's special! Waaay out of the box!

"Today, Africa has moved from a missionary receiving continent to a missionary sending continent. It is time for African Christians to celebrate God's goodness and respond to the mission realities of the 21ˢᵗ Century. The time has come for the African church to become a mission giving church."
~MISSIONS AFRICA TRUST FUND

I magine a headline in the world's most circulated international newspaper: "Africa Gives Millions of Dollars in Aid to America." "That will be the day," did you say?

For some this can only be a dream; for others, that would be a nightmare. What if I told you, I'm living this dream?

+35 TO -35

Ghana and Canada can be as different as being on two extreme ends of the thermometer. When my whole family and I arrived back in Canada on New Year's Day 2014 from a much-needed thawing trip to Ghana, we came from +35 Celsius weather straight into -35 weather. What a baptism!

But I was upbeat. Forget the weather. One of the major things that happened in Ghana was that Anyele and I held a novel Global Missions Breakfast which my dear brother (in-law) Franklin and sister Amma had graciously helped us put together at a hotel in a posh part of Accra.

Hosting a breakfast meeting per se was not the novelty. Ghanaian missionaries in North America presenting on what God was doing among international students in Canada and North America was maybe a bit more of an unfamiliarity.

But the real game changer was the stomach-churning (oh, did I say this was at breakfast?!) challenge to the African church thus, "If the mission has changed, and God is sending missionaries even from Africa to Canada (because that's what Anyele and I are), then not only should we send missionaries, we should be able to send the mission dollars to keep them there."

Seriously, this was a hit or miss situation. Since when did Africans start sending money to North America? Is the much-touted statistic rather not how many billions Africans send home from the West? In a recent article in *The Economist,* the writer states how "money sent home by relatives or friends working abroad—are the financial lifeblood of many poor countries. One of the biggest and fastest-growing markets is Africa, which received $32 billion in 2013. That is expected to grow to more than $40 billion by 2016."[257]

In fact, so entrenched is the mindset that the flow of funds should be from the West to Africa that in Ghana, for example, the typical money transfer agencies like Western Union and Moneygram, which together wield 50 percent of that market, don't even have a function whereby a Ghanaian can send money to the West! Read my lips: "You can't send money from Africa to America, duh!" You just can't. It's a "one-way street" operation!

This is way out of the box, *way* out of the window, making such a bold "God Ask" (as Steve Shadrach would put it) and expecting not to be ridiculed or put to shame. God, who is on the move, is good: we raised about 10,000 US dollars in Ghana that weekend for missions in Canada, as a result of that one meeting.

In fact, for the next few months, our biggest monthly supporter of our ISMC work (in dollar terms) was not even Canadian or American, it was an African—a Ghanaian living in Ghana, not earning dollars. But for the terrible depreciation of the Ghanaian cedi to the dollar in the first half of 2014 (value almost halved by the middle of the year!), he would have been the reigning Kingdom financier, for a much longer time. I am shaking my head right now: the mission has changed, indeed!

PACE-SETTING AFRICAN CHURCH

Many of those at the said breakfast were members of my home church in Ghana, the Legon Interdenominational Church (LIC), and got it. They got it because many of them, senior members of the University of Ghana in Legon, had themselves been international students and scholars in North America, Europe, Australia, and Japan. LIC was founded over thirty years ago to cater to the spiritual needs of lecturers of the University of Ghana and their families, and students.

Prof. Sefa-Dedeh, who himself attained his PhD from the University of Guelph in Canada many years ago, and was the founding dean of the engineering faculty of the University of Ghana, reiterated how LIC, as a campus church, should do much more to engage the nearly two-thousand international students from a few dozen countries. And he 'put his money where his mouth was.'

Some of the university's most senior leaders, including the registrar and pro-vice chancellor, are LIC congregants. The presiding elder then, who at the time of writing had just become a new pro-vice chancellor, commissioned his two deputies to meet with me on the way forward, at a follow-up visit in April, 2014.

The next thing I knew, I heard the awesome news that the Council of Elders had voted to support our ministry to international students in Canada with $6,000 annually, payable in two $3,000 truncheons each half year! *Unbelievable*! Totally out of the box!

You can imagine how shocked Canadians (and other Westerners) are whenever I tell them not only about my home church in Ghana supporting us in missions work, but by how much. At the time of writing, there was no church in Canada or the United States that had yet equaled this amount of support toward my ministry as ISMC president.

Just before this book went into print, another church in Accra, Ghana, the International Central Gospel Church Gbawe (Eagles Temple), wrote to inform me of their decision to support the mission to reach the world by reaching international students in Canada through ISMC by $1,000 yearly! God richly bless them and let them see much fruit from their phenomenal sacrifice!

NEW SENDING COUNTRIES, NEW MISSION MONEY

At the World Evangelical Alliance (WEA) Mission Commission's consultation in Izmir, Turkey, my main agenda as the representative leader of ISM in Canada was to join Leiton Chinn (Lausanne Senior Associate for ISM) and other ISM leaders from New Zealand, England, and South Africa, to get our newly-formed Lausanne ISM Global Leaders Network as an officially recognized mission network of the WEA's Mission Commission.

Of course, we also thoroughly enjoyed the plenaries, table group discussions, and the tour of the ancient city of Ephesus. One of the most soothing phrases I heard during the preliminaries was the term "new sending countries," referring to countries (mainly in the Global South) that are now the major thrust of missionary-sending.

Out of curiosity, I wandered into one of the small group sessions that was geared toward younger leaders; these emerging leaders in the room hailed from South Africa, Canada, Nigeria, and Scandinavia. We were beginning to warm up to each other and I was starting to enjoy the fellowship until one young man, one of the two Caucasian-Canadians in the room, either naïve or bigoted, said something like this: "Now with all the talk about the new missionary thrust coming from the Global South and them being the new sending countries, how are they going to do that when they are so poor and the wealth is over here in North America?!"

Huh?! I overreacted and could've easily gotten out of my seat and smacked him. Even though I did not—and he owes the Holy Spirit big time for producing the fruit of self-control in me at that moment—my violent jerk out of my seat must have been quite obvious. He must have perceived that had he been at arm's length I would have "laid hands on him." What he said was unfortunate, especially for a young Canadian Christian who was living today with a twentieth century imperialist, colonial mindset.

AFRICA'S NOT ALL BAD NEWS

I found the screaming headline (and corresponding eye-catching image) of a February 26, 2012, edition of *The Sunday Times Magazine* very interesting:

THE LION'S ROAR
Africa's economic boom. By John Aldridge.

Is this the same Africa that had been written off by the much-respected magazine *The Economist* in May, 2000, on its cover as "the hopeless continent"? At the turn of the new millennium, it was a damning catalog of wars, famines, and diseases. Alas, even *The Economist* had to do a U-turn eleven years on with a different magazine cover, singing a totally different tune: "Africa rising."

It is true I am African and proud. Yet this chapter is not meant to sing Africa's praises but just to say, if God says it's time for Africa to push missions, the God who could turn Samaria's captivity around in twenty-four hours can do the same with Africa.[258] Nothing gets in the way of *Missio Dei*, the mission of God. John Aldridge's article was very upbeat:

> The scale and extent of Africa's economic boom is unprecedented—albeit from a barrel-scrapingly low base. Over the last decade, six of the world's 10 fastest-growing countries were African. In eight of the last 10 years, Africa's lion states have grown faster than Asia's tigers. The fastest growing economy in the world last year was Ghana—at a whopping 13%, compared with barely 1% in most European countries and just over 1% in America. The International Monetary Fund (IMF) expects Africa to grow by nearly 6% this year, the same as last year, with average income in economic leaders such as Nigeria expected to triple by 2030.

> If that isn't impressive enough, how about this for an economic indicator? Thanks to debt relief in Africa and the borrowing splurge in Europe, many European countries are now more indebted than African nations. Oil-rich Angola is even lending cash to its old colonial master, Portugal. New African billionaires and multimillionaires are being minted at such a rate that a few months ago Forbes magazine, the bible of the global business elite, published its inaugural list of the "40 richest Africans," which it called "a testament to the growing global importance of the continent."

What's more, the wealth is trickling down. Africa now has the fastest-growing middle class in the world. Some 313m people. 34% of the continent's population, spend $2.20 a day, a 100% rise in less than 20 years, according to the African Development Bank (AfDB). By 2060, the number of middle-class Africans will grow to 1.1 billion (42% of the predicted population), the AfDB says. By then, those living below the poverty line will be in the minority—33%.[259]

"Overall foreign investment in Africa has grown more than sixfold in the last decade. Investment by Chinese firms alone has increased tenfold," the article continues elsewhere. Why not? After all, the rate of return on foreign investment in Africa is higher than any other developing region, McKinsey reveals.[260] "Africans themselves don't need numbers to confirm that their time is now. They can feel it. Many who left their homeland in search of a better life in the west are now returning."[261]

Oh, boy, do we still have problems; and who doesn't? I guess you are too familiar with them so I don't need to elaborate. That's all there is on the news anyway. I just thought I'd give you another side; the untold side of the story.

So could God use Africa—even Africa—to send forth missionaries and mission dollars into all the world? You had better believe it; even if it means *thinking outside the window.*

WHAT YOU MAY NOT KNOW ABOUT AFRICA

"Africa is a multi-faceted and fascinating continent. With so many different ethnicities and nationalities, one common practice unites all Africans: a culture of giving. Philanthropy, or giving, has long been practiced in Africa."[262] For some who are reading this and have never known Africa except for the European headlines and American cable news, you may find that shocking.

You know what else you will find in the foreword of this UBS-Trust Africa collaborative research entitled "Africa's Wealthy Give Back Report"?

> Over the past ten to fifteen years, there has been a phenom-
> enal growth in philanthropic institutions across Africa, and
> the informal traditions of individual giving have not dimin-
> ished. Hence, the vehicle is not broken and neither has it
> slowed down—if anything, it has gathered speed in the
> right direction—and that is precisely the reason we must
> give it greater and more careful attention. We need to know
> more and understand better what fuels it, how its compo-
> nent parts fit together, why it runs the way it does, and what
> else it needs in order to continue to run on its own steam.[263]

If the global Church would stop crippling Africa by only giving aid, and rather help her develop the kinds of systems, structures, and processes of distilling resources for philanthropy that the West has mastered, the whole world and the whole Church will be the better for it—we will all win.

That is why I love the idea of the Missions Africa Trust Fund and what the Global Generosity Network is doing to make it a reality.

MISSIONS AFRICA TRUST FUND

Nana Yaw Offei-Awuku, my good friend and namesake, Lausanne International Deputy Director for English and Portuguese-speaking Africa, not too long ago launched the Missions Africa Trust Fund, an indigenous African initiative as a direct response to the Cape Town Commitment of the third Lausanne Conference on World Evangelization in 2010.

To put things in perspective, he sets a good historical context to this:

100 years ago at the first World Missions Conference in Edinburgh in 1910, Africa was mostly unreached with the Gospel. Many Western missionaries obeyed God's call to the mission fields of Africa, some died for the sake of the Gospel. These missionaries were supported by the sacrificial giving of Christians in their home countries. Today, Africa has moved from a missionary receiving continent to a missionary sending continent. It is time for African Christians to celebrate God's goodness and respond to the mission realities of the 21st Century. The time has come for the African church to become a mission giving church.[264]

The concept of the Missions Africa Trust Fund (MATF) was born in November, 2011, to raise financial support for mission initiatives from within Africa. After nearly three years of prayer and discussions, the MATF was launched in 2014 as an African mission-giving initiative. As a collaborative African initiative, the MATF will facilitate giving to strategic mission initiatives related to the Lausanne Movement, churches, mission networks, and ministries across Africa.

Vision: Mobilizing resources to support the whole Church to take the whole Gospel to the whole Africa and beyond.

Mission: The Missions Africa Trust Fund is a Christian investment and charity foundation with a strategic focus on mobilizing and multiplying resources from Africa and elsewhere to support Kingdom mission initiatives in Africa and from Africa to the rest of the world.

Stakeholder Statement: The MATF is an initiative of the Lausanne Movement, inspired and independently governed by African church and mission leaders, in partnership with the Global Generosity Network.

I believe with Nana Yaw that, "God is at work in challenging the African church to become a 21st Century example of a mission giving church—as Africa moves from a 'missionary receiving' to 'missionary sending' continent. We are passionate to see this vision become a reality in spite of the current situation."[265]

WHAT YOU DON'T KNOW WILL KILL YOU

I believe that key, mainly Christian, countries like Ghana, Kenya and Uganda all of a sudden discovering oil is not an accident.

If a mission-sending continent is God's *vision*, then *He* has already made the pro*vision*. Nobody's parochial interest will stop God from what He wants to do. It's not about north, south, east, or west: it's about *God's Kingdom* coming on the *whole* earth as it is in heaven!

If we're going to roll with God, our chief allegiance should not be to our continents, nations, tribes, or tongues (and certainly not our (neo)colonialist agenda), but to *His* Kingdom and *His* agenda.

OH, WOW!

I recently had the privilege of being the plenary speaker at Prairie Bible Institute's Christian Life Week. On our way to lunch on one of the afternoons, the president of the school, Mark Maxwell (grandson of the founding principal L.E. Maxwell) and I bumped into the professor of Christian mission and intercultural studies. The former thought it was imperative that we arrange to have a lunch meeting a couple of days later. We did. I'm mighty glad we did.

Not only did I thoroughly enjoy Emma's God story, her philosophy of ministry, and her sheer pleasantness, but something she revealed greatly piqued my interest when the issue of how the mission has so changed, including the flow of mission dollars, came up. We laughed, yes, but it is a serious matter: that the majority of funds (70 percent) a certain Canadian agency in Mozambique receives is not from Canada. It comes from Brazil!

Whoever thought that funds would flow from the Global South to oil the wheels of the glorious Gospel of Jesus Christ *everywhere*?

MONEY COMETH!

The plenary speaker during our Montreal Chinese Alliance Grace Church's 2014 annual missions conference was a former Toronto pastor who now divides his time between Hong Kong and mainland China, raising a missionary force among (what he estimates as) the seventy-million Christians in China. In fact, should the growth trend of the Gospel continue in China, it just might overtake the United States as the country with the most evangelical Christians within the next couple of decades.

And these missionaries are going everywhere, including dangerous Islamic territories. As the figures and statistics continued to marinate in my spirit, after a few days it occurred to me that the most powerful emerging economies of the world (first nick-named "BRIC" by economist Jim O'Neill of Goldman Sachs in 2001 in a paper titled "Building Better Global Economic BRICs"—and now it's stuck) may also hold the key to the growth of the Gospel both in people and financial resources: Brazil, Russia, India, and China. South Africa was later added in 2011 to form BRICS. These are both the fastest growing and largest emerging market economies, accounting for nearly half of the total population of the world!

It is only a matter of time that China, which is now the world's second largest economy and the world's largest creditor, may overtake the United States to become number one. 'Everyone' knows that by 2030 Asia will be the world's socioeconomic powerhouse as it was some six centuries ago. This has *huge* implications for the Gospel of Jesus Christ!

Have you noticed that all the BRICS countries (except Russia) are in the Global South, which we mentioned in Chapter Two as where the most

Gospel action in the world is today, where the mission swell is only beginning? Is this a coincidence?

DIASPORA DIMENSION

And in all this, I haven't even touched on the African diaspora—those people from Africa now settled overseas, but still maintaining strong ties to their countries. Don't forget they are the ones that remit over $30 billion a year to their motherland.[266] Will they not support missions in the West also if they were given a vision of that and shown how they could?

At the time of writing, all my monthly support coming from the United States to Canada (through our sister ministry, International Students Inc.), was entirely coming from Ghanaian professionals in the diaspora.

How about the multiple millions of other diaspora people the world over from the Global South who are of strong Christian, even evangelical, persuasion?

MISSIONARIES DIDN'T TRAIN US

It is rare to find an African missionary properly trained in the art of fundraising; I shan't belabour the point in the previous chapter. *Thinking outside the window* in the training of African missionaries now, should absolutely include how to raise funds locally; not just wait for handouts from abroad. Again, our help comes from *above*; not *abroad*!

GOD WILL DO ANYTHING

God will stop at *nothing* (within His character and nature) to manifest His love for us; even sacrificing His own Son. If He would do that, what makes you think He will not use any means possible to get the word out. It is true that the majority of giving to missions currently still comes from the West. God can keep using that or choose to look elsewhere.

God will do anything to save souls. He will use the wealthy like Joseph of Arimathea, and the dirt poor alike. I've never, for the life of me, figured out why, when God wanted to lend missionary support to the itinerant prophet Elijah, He bypassed all the wealthy and went for a poor widow and her son about to die after their last meal.

I pray my Western brothers and sisters will never be bypassed by God in His great missionary enterprise today, but if Israel could be sidestepped by God, anyone can. We had better be wary of pride. And this goes for the Church in the Majority World as well, lest we go about shoulder-tapping as if we did anything.

God will use anyone and anything at any time to reach everyone everywhere, irrespective of cardinal point or net worth. Dr. Ralph Winter's work chillingly illustrates this:

> How hard have we tried to save others? Consider the fact that the U.S. evangelical slogan, "Pray, give or go" allows people merely to pray, if that is their choice! By contrast the Friends Missionary Prayer Band of South India numbers 8,000 people in their prayer bands and supports 80 full-time missionaries in North India. If my denomination (with its unbelievably greater wealth per person) were to do that well, we would not be sending 500 missionaries, but 26,000. In spite of their true poverty, those poor people in South India are sending 50 times as many cross-cultural missionaries as we are."[267]

The recent UBS Report on Philanthropy in Africa already cited involved one hundred wealthy Africans, which for the purpose of the study was defined as individuals earning more than USD 150,000 annually or with USD 500,000 in investible assets. God may use some of these wealthy people; or none of them. *He is God*! The God of the mission. He does whatever pleases Him.

LITTLE AFRICAN GIRL WHO GAVE HER ALL

He said, "The plain truth is that this widow has given by far the largest offering today. All these others made offerings that they'll never miss; she gave extravagantly what she couldn't afford—she gave her all."[268]

Those were the words of Jesus, when a poor widow gave her last copper coins (mite), which has now become the proverbial "widow's mite." She gave her all. What a challenge to think that *God not only looks at how much we give but also how much is left.*

Similarly, fast-forward eighteen-hundred years later: the story of Mary Jones has always intrigued and inspired me. That a little nine-year-old Welsh girl who had just given her life to Christ and longed for her own copy of the Bible, will save for six years and walk twenty-five miles to go get it! Even then all of the copies of the sole seller in Bala were either sold or spoken for. Mary wept in despair. Not only did her distress so profoundly touch Mr. Thomas Charles such that he gave her a copy which was else-bound, but something historic happened.

"Mary's visit profoundly impacted Thomas Charles. He began to wonder what could be done for others such as Mary—for people who long for the Bible around the world. He proposed to the Council of the Religious Tract Society to form a new Society to supply Wales with Bibles. And, in 1804, the British and Foreign Bible Society was established in London."[269] The rest is history. Today, there are 146 Bible societies operating in over two hundred countries and territories under the banner of "The United Bible Societies."[270]

Fast-forward two hundred years later: another story of a female and money, another young girl; only this time in Africa. While in Ghana in May 2014, during my last week, I held a number of ISMC-related meetings of all sorts, including one with the SIM Ghana director, conferring with leaders of the most influential "on campus" church in the nation, phone conversations with the president of the Ghana-Canada Chamber of Commerce, etc.

The last, on the morning of 1st May, was a breakfast meeting on the pristine Akuapem mountains to cast vision about how *God is on the move* regarding international students. The breakfast was sumptuous—all donated by Patrick and Vivian, the proprietors of the venue, Hephzibah Christian Retreat Centre—and the "upper room" was jam-packed with Africans eager to know what God was doing in global mission today, and even more eager to partake in it.

All of this was good, but nothing prepared me for what was about to happen right after we were done. Patrick came to tell me that his daughter had conscripted her friends to join her in counting coins she wanted to donate to global mission! This sounded cute, but the full impact of that had still not hit me quite yet.

Not long after, Abbie came bearing a heavy brown envelope with the inscriptions "To: ISMC" and "GHC 78." Now, she had my full attention.

What had happened was that Abbie had been so touched by the urgency of God's global mission and how He is calling the African church into active participation that she had decided to break open her piggy bank and give **all** of its contents to missions.

Apparently, she couldn't even find the key to her treasure so she had looked for a hammer to break it open and count out all her coins with her friends. Abbie gave her all, literally. She had been saving these coins since age six; she was now fourteen. Due to the Ghanaian cedi doing very poorly against the dollar, Abbie's gift was worth "only" $28, but like the widow Jesus glowingly spoke about in Luke 21, though the economic value of her coins wasn't much, she gave by far the *largest* offering because she gave her *all*.

Abbie's inspirational story reminds me so much of Mary Jones, the nine-year old girl alluded to above who saved for six years and walked twenty-five miles to be able to get a Bible of her own—a story which inspired the founding of the Bible societies now all around the world. Who knows what this African girl's story will also inspire? Incidentally, just the day before, using the story of twelve-year-old Samuel, I had spoken to the children in Abbie's *Liberty American School* in Accra about how *"Our big God can do great things with little people who will humbly listen and obey."* Who knows? As I travel the world raising funds and friends for the critical and strategic work of ISMC, sometimes I carry these coins along to inspire others and make my point.

Remember that *God doesn't just look at how much we give; He also looks at how much is left!* You too may not have much (time, money, strength, talents or volunteers), but are you giving your *all*?

LIFE LESSON FROM PAPA CHANG

The same "dirt-poor" African continent has firms like South African mobile provider MTN, which operates in twenty-three African countries and makes about $2 million an hour in Nigeria alone.[271] India has some of the poorest of the poor, and yet boasts also of some of the richest of the rich. The wealthy Western world that gives so much in aid and to missions also has some of the poorest people I've ever met in my life, especially the homeless in major cities. How about that?

When I was a World Vision Youth Ambassador, one of the most valuable life lessons I learned from the late Papa Chang, founder of the program, who was then CEO of World Vision Taiwan, was this: *nobody is too poor to give; nobody is too rich to receive.*

Africa is giving money to global mission today—you had better believe it. It's not just a dream!

Now, let's talk about *your* dream.

---

*"Depend on it. God's work done in God's way will never lack God's supply.
He is too wise a God to frustrate His purposes for lack of funds,
and He can just as easily supply them ahead of time as afterwards,
and He much prefers doing so."*
~ JAMES HUDSON TAYLOR

~15~

"Give Up Your Small Ambitions"

It really is a pathetic box you live in!

"You can do something other than working with God in His purpose,
but it will always be something lesser,
and you couldn't come up with something better."
~Steve Hawthorne

DON'T ASK ME WHY

I sat across from this busy Marriot hotel manager at a restaurant in the heart of downtown Toronto. This was a young Ghanaian woman who has done quite well for herself in Canada. Though on the surface it seemed like all that was on the table was just dinner, I sensed there was more.

Finally she gathered the courage to say what many wonder but are never willing or able to ask, "Why would you leave your awesome life in Ghana to be here?" Good question, my friend, good question!

Many people have not understood many things about me, especially most recently why I would leave a profession like medicine or forsake a great life in Ghana for Canada. Even I haven't understood sometimes, but for God.

Sometimes people have said very hurtful things, most of which I'm glad I never get to hear in person. Remember the POS award I mentioned earlier in Chapter Three, given to me in the presence of many Ghanaian dignitaries, including ministers of state and the chief justice? I once had the privilege of hosting the founder/CEO of the organizers of that event when he came to Atlantic Canada for a short course.

As he sat in the passenger's side and I drove on, he, too, finally gathered the courage to ask, "So Doc, how are you surviving here?" He was obviously referring to how I was making ends meet without practicing medicine (and he really couldn't tell what I was doing in its stead either!) and having to take care of a wife (in school or in limbo?) and three children then. He revealed to me something I had never even imagined, but pierced my soul. Apparently, there were rumors in Ghana that my wealthy mother (I honestly don't know where she keeps all her alleged wealth!) was sending me money from Ghana for my upkeep in Canada! In other words, I was on "welfare," albeit from family. Imagine! And this was long before mission support even started coming to ISMC from Ghana!

"HE NOT TOO SURE"

But nothing cut me to the heart like a one-liner in an email of 13 August, 2009. And it wasn't even to me. What had happened was that barely a month after we had arrived in Canada to settle, my father sent an email informing me of his impending visit to Toronto for an International Needs board meeting.

He had an old high school friend in Ottawa, Uncle Meiz, that he really wanted to connect with and was hoping we could drive together to see him when he (Dad) visited us in Montreal, since Ottawa is barely two hours away.

The introduction and planning in the latter email of September 10, 2009, all seemed well and good until I decided to skim through the earlier email thread.

We had left Ghana on August 19, 2009. The email of August 13 (only sent to Uncle Meiz), obviously had preceded our landing in Canada and clearly anticipated our arrival here. Part of it read (unedited):

> My son and his family would be relocating in Montreal next week. She doing a PhD. He not too sure. Young Perbi schooling and being "toddler-assisted."

Anyele had a purpose for coming to Canada; even two-year-old Agyina had something definite to do, but *the man of the house* had none? I know my Dad and love him with all my heart. In April 2015, I flew all the way back to Ghana from Canada just to honour him as he celebrated his sixty-fifth birthday and retirement from KMPG, one of the world's top four accounting firms, as deputy senior partner. It was sobering to hear tribute after tribute regarding his humility, integrity, professional excellence, simplicity, attention to detail, discipline, love, Christian faith etc. from professional colleagues and the Christian community alike. Above all, from his own dear wife (my professor-mother) and all of us four children. Indeed, I have read and interacted with many world-class leaders but no one has modeled integrity for me like my own father, Reindorf Baah Perbi.

So I do not think he meant that phrase, "He not too sure," for harm. He was vocalizing something many people were sensing but couldn't, or wouldn't, articulate. I had always been an ambitious, passionate, purpose-driven, goal-oriented young man, and for me this was the worst thing anybody could think of me, especially coming from my own father: "He not too sure."

DOCTOR DIES

You read of my "Death Day." That tragic accident was, of course, in the Ivorian newspapers: "Un soldat de l'Onuci tué dans un accident." But really it wasn't just one soldier; all three died, two physically, and the third, myself, in a sort of metaphysical way.

I knew I had been spared by the awesome hand of God for a purpose beyond medicine (only part of which has still been revealed to date, even in this book). When people have wondered why on earth I would give up such a lucrative and respectable profession like medicine to become whatever I am now, it is only because they haven't died like I did.

I doff my hat to my parents who sacrificed everything to ensure I had the best of education. It hasn't been easy on them—to reckon with the fact that the son of whom they so boast, the doctor, is no longer practicing "the noble profession."

I remember one day having to gather the nerve to respectfully say to my dear father, "Dad, your son the doctor is dead." Indeed! I died. The Doc is no more. "I have been crucified with Christ and I no longer live..."[272]

"FROM A RARE HEIGHT"

I have always wanted to be a missionary, a bearer of the glorious Gospel of Jesus Christ that changes lives. I just didn't want to make a career out of it, or be a poor one at that. In fact, apart from a few minor, non-eternal perks that come with being a doctor, the major reason I pursued medicine was so I could reach people with the love and message of the Gospel of Jesus Christ. I always felt that being a doctor and interacting with people at the most vulnerable point of their lives would be a great segue into a salvation conversation.

There are many reasons why God moved me along the path of medicine (and who knows, I just might practice again someday as a resurrected doc!)

but I find it amusing how He still brought me to "the end in mind:" one who bears the message of hope that changes this *ephemeral* world and saves souls for the *eternal*. Medicine was a piece; not *the* puzzle.

I'm so reminded of the powerful words of the renowned African writer, Ben Okri, who was himself at one-time a Nigerian international student in the United Kingdom: "*We plan our lives according to a dream that came to us in our childhood, and we find that life alters our plans. And yet, at the end, from a rare height, we also see that our dream was our fate. It's just that providence had other ideas as to how we would get there. Destiny plans a different route, or turns the dream around, as if it were a riddle, and fulfils the dream in ways we couldn't have expected.*"

OF PLOWS, PEOPLE AND PULPITS!

> "*When you live the committed life of God,*
> *you will upset a lot of people, but no plow has ever done its job*
> *without upsetting the earth.*"

Those were words that one mysterious Nasir whispered into the ears of an injured American soldier lying flat on his back in the deserts of Afghanistan. Though a work of fiction, a lot of the story line in *Gifts of the Heart* is obviously crafted after the life of its writer, Ghanaian-American heart surgeon, Dr. Hassan A. Tetteh. Let me tell you how this upsetting plow showed up from the pulpit one day.

It was a fine Sunday morning and I was doing my usual: sharing the Word of God. While I was preaching up a storm at a church in the Greater Toronto Area, I couldn't help but notice from the pulpit a dark, bespectacled, distinguished, middle-aged gentleman who was looking rather intently at me. Then at times he would just bow his head, obviously in deep emotion, but of which kind I couldn't quite tell.

It was not until after the service was over that we got to interact and I had a shock of my life. This man knew me from Ghana! "I was even at your wedding," he told me, "at the invitation of your father-in-law." Apparently, this man had been one of my worst critics when he heard I had jumped ship, *MV Medicine*. His wife is a doctor, too, and seeing how life-saving, even miraculous, this noble profession is first-hand, he could not fathom why anyone in his right senses who had this kind of privilege would give it up *just to preach!* I had made a commitment to ministry and mission full-time, put my hands to the plow, and someone somewhere, whose first-name I didn't even know, was upset?

That morning he was profoundly touched and transformed. He was more or less undergoing a divine heart transplant as I spoke the Word of God with the power of His anointing. If I ever needed an OK, even a commissioning, from my adversaries to function in my God-given calling, that day I had it. "Young man," he said, "go on doing what you are doing. Keep on preaching the Gospel. Don't you ever listen to people like me who don't understand! This is really your calling!"

"Thanks, sir, but no thanks." I *know* this is my calling. *I'm* that one who died, remember? And I didn't need his (or any other person's) approval, blessing, or affirmation, but it was still nice to see that, "When a man's ways please the Lord, he makes even his enemies to be at peace with him."[273]

Hear the voice of Nasir again, *"When you live the committed life of God, you will upset a lot of people, but no plow has ever done its job without upsetting the earth."* And now hear the even higher voice of Jesus, the Master Himself, *"No one who puts a hand to the plow and looks back is fit for service in the kingdom of God."*[274] Let my pulpit-plow upset the peoples of the earth, but for me there *is no turning back, no turning back.*

And as you shall soon see, these "light and momentary troubles" are nothing compared with the glory ahead, earthly and eternal.

FROM PUNY TO PENTHOUSE

You would think that having obeyed God in an epoch way once, it would always be easy to subsequently. Sure, sometimes, in some ways; but certainly not always. Every day is a new challenge to respond to His fresh callings and commands.

God indeed has an amazing sense of humor. He invades our lives, challenges us to give up what we're used to (or becoming used to) and says, "Let it all go and come for a ride!" If you are like me, you sometimes resist, kick and scream, finally yield, and in the end, wonder why you hadn't given up your teeny-weeny puny dreams and desires, goals, and go-gets earlier!

When I finally accepted the call to serve as president of ISMC, I agreed to take office in May, 2013. Obviously I had to round up my financial advisory practice of nearly two-and-a-half years at Investors Group. One of my immediate internal conflicts was that I had worked hard to qualify for an all-expenses-paid business training program at our corporate headquarters in Winnipeg. Hitherto I had never been to the city of Winnipeg nor visited our magnificent 447 Portage Avenue edifice.

Arrrggghhh! Why now?! My impending move to ISMC wasn't public knowledge by this time and I was really tempted to take full advantage of this IG opportunity and resign the week after (or so). But my conscience wouldn't let me. Was it really fair to let IG invest all these resources in me and then just quit? Another part of me said, "But you've earned it! Besides, it's only a small portion of the hundreds of thousands of dollars you've brought to the organization anyway!" My chief concern was my Christian witness: "So he knew he had another offer and was going to quit and yet made us go through all this trouble of investing in him? Cheapskate! Cheat!...and he calls himself a Christian!"

I decided to let it go. I had a higher calling. You wouldn't believe what I'm about to tell you. Barely six months after this episode, I was in Winnipeg alright, and got to visit the IG headquarters too. Cool! You know the best part? I wasn't with the rank and file of IG staff and consultants. I went straight up to the corner office of the president of Investors Group, Murray Taylor, and had lunch with him and his cherished wife Charlotte, as president of ISMC!

THE BEST $6 EVER INVESTED

You see, what had happened was this: Rick Wilgosh, my amazing Kelowna city director, is very good friends with Murray Taylor; in fact, Murray was his best man at his wedding. It was he who had arranged this incredible meeting with Murray and Charlotte.

I so clearly remember that Winnipeg morning when we pulled into a nearby public underground parking lot in Rick's truck and had to pay for our spot. I quickly pulled out my wallet to do so before he could even attempt to reach his. It cost us $6 and I remember Rick saying in jest, "This may very well be the best six dollars you've ever invested!" And it was.

Not only was there the invaluable time with one of Canada's most respected CEOs, the food was out of this world, and the discussions so stimulating. Through their foundation, the Taylors invested tens-of-thousands of dollars towards our expansion efforts at ISMC. The best $6 ever invested, indeed! ROI, incredible!

In hindsight, imagine if I had held on to my "earned," "it's-my-right" IG trip to Winnipeg—how would that compare with this glorious personal meeting with Murray and Charlotte? And meeting as president-to-president for that matter; not one of his "common floor members," so-to-speak. Imagine if I had refrained from letting $6 go, compared to the tens-of-thousands of dollars in return, and the incalculable experiences mentioned.

These are "light and momentary" examples of what a ridiculous shooting in the foot we do to ourselves when we do not give up our puny, "small ambitions" for God's grander visions! Get out of your box!

PhD GOES BUST!

Do you remember that awesome conversation with Anyele on August 20, 2009, when we landed in Montreal, tired, hungry, and highly inflammable? How Anyele basically said, "You didn't follow me here; I'm not the reason you've come to Canada. God brought you here for His greater purposes, far beyond me"?

Well, how prophetic! Within a few weeks of arriving in Canada I had the joy of attending Anyele's graduation ceremony for her Master's in Economics. Meanwhile she had already gotten into the PhD program. And having taken many of the requisite courses already at the Master's level she had a huge head start. Or at least so we thought.

Then within a year of arriving in Canada and plunging into the PhD she was out of the program! What? I thought *that* was the reason we moved here in the first place? Yes? Well, no!

Through a set of incredible circumstances—some outright bizarre—she had finally been asked to withdraw from the program! What? First of all, she was not particularly enjoying the course, at all, which seemed strange for someone who had done economics at the undergrad level (graduated with first class honors) and had gone on to pursue the same at the Master's level. She struggled and stumbled through the course, even wondering about the whole purpose of pursuing this PhD in the first place.

Then in addition, we got pregnant with our second child. That, under normal circumstances shouldn't be an issue because Anyele typically has uneventful trimesters and even painless deliveries (that's a miracle for another book!). So what made this pregnancy an issue was the fact that she was in an academic environment where it seemed an unspoken taboo to get pregnant if you were a serious student!

She still worked hard. In fact, I clearly recollect her going down to the faculty to run a seminar only four days after she had delivered Nana Ashede! At that time we didn't even have a car—she went by Metro.

So finally Anyele writes her comprehensive exams[275]... and fails! What? Hitherto, failing in university was an unknown, unfamiliar territory to her! Well, we consoled ourselves that since she had another chance to re-write the exam we would take this in our stride.

But even before she could regroup and retake the exam, two very bizarre things happened. First, one of her professors called her aside and asked her, "Really, why do you want to do a PhD?" There's no need to divulge the detailed content of this nonsensical conversation, except to say he basically was stating that there was no need to retake the exam; she wouldn't pass. In fact, we have a friend in the student government who had wanted us to pursue this matter or even sue! We let it go. We were therefore not surprised, but still very hurt, when she retook the exam and apparently failed again.

The most bizarre thing in all of this *telenovela*-like drama was that Anyele's professor who was funding her suddenly died! The late Prof. McKinnon had been funding Anyele as her research assistant, and that project money, plus what she made as a teaching assistant, was all the "student money" we were living on.

The good professor, in September 2009, began her sabbatical and left for Australia. She returned to Montreal on Christmas vacation only to be suddenly diagnosed with advanced uterine cancer. This single, childless academic stalwart immediately underwent emergency surgery and began chemotherapy and radiation therapy—all to no avail. She died within seven months, just before Anyele retook the comprehensive exams. Just like that!

This had several implications, the most obvious and immediate being that there was no money to fund Anyele! And don't forget this was still around the height of the global economic crisis of 2008/09. McGill was struggling with funding, as were many universities, and it stood to reason that Anyele be asked to withdraw.

These are the reasons why, after barely a year in Canada, the apparent "human reason" we came to the country (to pursue a PhD) had fallen apart. But we clearly see the divine hand of Providence today. God used the length of a PhD program to draw me into the country (I knew a PhD took *forever* and I wasn't prepared to keep the family apart any further). After He got me out of Africa into Canada for a "good enough reason," in my human opinion, then He closed the door.

It may surprise you to learn that, actually, the "human reason" why we had thought it would be a good thing for Anyele to pursue this PhD was so she could remain in academia to have access to young people—our passion, our calling, our life! God kept the vision, His vision of using us to impact young people alright, but had a different methodology in mind.

The Lord had shown us He could use me as a missionary without medicine; and now was about to prove that He could also offer us access to university students without a PhD in economics either.

Today, there's almost no university in Canada that we haven't spoken at. My staff and I at ISMC get to connect with over twenty-thousand international students every year from the Pacific to the Atlantic! God had a better plan in mind.

A far better plan, especially considering that most of Anyele's colleagues in the same PhD program hadn't completed by the time we had already began this nationwide and global impact through ISMC. And now getting tenure as a university professor has become such an endangered species that many of her contemporaries have become "permanent professional students," pursuing one degree after the other, one post-doctoral fellowship after another in the wilderness of *no work*!

Not only have we been amazed at the phenomenon of PhDs not finding work in academia, we have been shocked at how restricted even those who do are in being able to vocalize their faith on campus in Canada.

God, indeed, is the God that declares the end from the beginning! We are doing exactly what we set out to do, without the tool which we thought we would use, but God knew would do us less good. We had our plan, a good plan, but God had a much better one in mind—the best plan!

PRAIRIES TO SCANDINAVIA

Mark Maxwell, president of Prairie Bible Institute (PBI) in Three Hills, Alberta, and his dear wife Elaine, reached out to me after reading of my taking on the leadership of ISMC in *Faith Today*.[276] We have since developed a wonderful friendship in life and partnership in ministry.

For three mornings in September 2014, when I had the joy of being the plenary speaker at PBI's Christian Life Week, one of my key challenges to the young people, as we shared from the third chapter of Paul's letter to the Philippians, was to "give up the good stuff" they had in mind or were holding on to, and take hold of the "God stuff."

Apostle Paul thought he had it good (and he lists all the "good stuff" from his family pedigree to his professional degree) and then shockingly throws it all down and calls it "dung!" "rubbish!"

Not that staying in Ghana and making it as a young doctor wasn't a good thing; not that working with the United Nations isn't a good thing; really, what's wrong with a PhD in economics? That's not the point. The point is, many times the enemy of the *best* that God has for us is the *good* we grab for ourselves!

In the light of God's best for us, we eventually see that our good does not only *not* look good enough, it looks like a loss, and it is rubbish!

I trust from sharing a bit of our journey with you, it goes without saying that it hasn't been an easy road. We weren't exactly laughing when we set off for Canada with little money and no job, neither did we throw a party when Anyele had to exit the PhD program!

But let me tell you, if you really want to live out God's best for your life, it will inconvenience you! Or so it may seem at the time. When I preached "The Inconvenience of Christmas" during Christmas 2013, the message didn't quite go viral on YouTube, but it certainly made a few dozen hits on almost every continent. Even one of my mentees in Norway got many of her church friends there to listen to it online.

The main point was that we always talk about Mary, Joseph, and the Christmas story in such glowing terms, but not many have ever stopped to think just how *inconvenient* this must have been for Mary and Joseph—especially Mary!

Do you not think she had her thirty-year plan for her life? Do you suppose all along she had wanted her firstborn child to be called "Jesus" and "out of wedlock?" Can you imagine how it felt to be misunderstood by everyone—pregnant on your own? Or worse still, pregnant *by God*?! Whoever heard of such anathema! All because God had some super-duper six thousand-year plan for humanity which He was about to deploy and His favor had located a young teenager in Nazareth, a town in Galilee, Israel?

We could say this teenage girl's life was totally messed up by God! And you call that *favour*? Indeed, Angel Gabriel...indeed! Come again? But see what that attitude of surrender Mary had has wrought for us all with the conception, birth, life, and ministry, death, burial, resurrection, and ascension of the Lord Jesus Christ?

Just because Mary accepted the inconvenience of Christmas, today we have the opportunity and audacity to believe in her son, God's Son, knowing, "Salvation is found in no one else, for there is no other name under heaven given to mankind by which we must be saved."[277]

My wife and I are glad today that we accepted all the "inconveniences" that moving to Canada from our cozy lives in Africa has brought. We had no idea that today we'd be Africans pastoring an *English*-speaking *Chinese* church in a *French* city in North America. There wasn't a precedent; neither did we even have the mental framework to conceive such a thing! Totally *out of the box!* We had *no idea* He was going to thrust us right in the *center* of His amazing global phenomenon today of the missionary force moving from everywhere to everywhere!

How could we have envisaged that He would call us to lead a staff of about 110 (80 percent of whom are older than us; and by the way none of the staff was Black when we joined!) to reach tens of thousands of international students each year in the second widest country on earth!

How on earth could I have perceived that the experience, wisdom, talents, and personality of an African would be treasured on the board of Jews for Jesus Canada? Jews for Jesus?! Oh, my, *outside the window!*

FULL CIRCLE: BACK TO LAUSANNE

We've come full circle. Remember that I spent a considerable amount of space in the earlier chapters of this book on the history of the Lausanne Movement and its implications for missions then and now? And how through a Lausanne Younger Leaders Gathering in Malaysia the Lord would change the trajectory of my life forever?

Well, in February of 2014, I was shocked to discover my name in a Lausanne press release. Quite honestly, I had seen the email, among several others in regards to the next Younger Leaders Gathering that had originally been planned for Kiev in 2015 (prior to the Ukraine political crisis), and hadn't even bothered to delve into this particular email.

It was my good friend, Nana Yaw Offei-Awuku, Lausanne International Deputy Director for English and Portuguese-Speaking Africa, who brought my name in the document to my attention. I woke up that morning to the very pleasant and absolutely humbling surprise of finding my name in the Lausanne Movement's February 17 press release among "Kingdom greats" like Ramez Atallah, Aijith Fernando, Peter Kuzmic, and John Piper!

Founded by Billy Graham and cemented by the likes of John Stott, since 1974 when the Lausanne Movement speaks, people listen. Lausanne had just aptly described my International Student Ministries of Canada (ISMC) presidency as a *"strategic global leadership role."* Like David, I couldn't help but cry out: "Who am I, Sovereign Lord, and what is my family, that you have brought me this far?"[278] And to think that all of this *almost* never happened...because I had my own puny, "small ambitions" that I thought so highly of!

*"My thoughts are nothing like your thoughts," says the LORD.
"And my ways are far beyond anything you could imagine. For
just as the heavens are higher than the earth, so my ways are
higher than your ways and my thoughts higher than your
thoughts."*[279]

May I throw a personal challenge to you too? Whatever "good" dream,
plan, or ambition you may be holding on to that God is asking you to release
for His best, do it! *Just do it*! In the words of sixteenth century missionary
Francis Xavier, you too must *"Give up your small ambitions!"* God is thinking
outside, *way* outside, of your narrow window!

"I NEVER MADE A SACRIFICE"

David Livingstone was born 165 years before me in the same month of
March. Like me, he was a medical doctor. He was a missionary in his era; so
am I in mine. He came to my backyard in Africa; I'm returning the favor by
coming to his in the West.

People thought he had made an incredible sacrifice of his life—an
Englishman choosing to live in and never leave primitive Africa as a mis-
sionary all his life. His direct response to that notion is evident in his
December 4, 1857, stirring appeal to the students of Cambridge University
(I bet there were a few international students sprinkled among them):

> For my own part, I have never ceased to rejoice that God
> has appointed me to such an office. People talk of the sac-
> rifice I have made in spending so much of my life in Africa.
> Can that be called a sacrifice which is simply paid back as a
> small part of a great debt owing to our God, which we can
> never repay? Is that a sacrifice which brings its own blest
> reward in healthful activity, the consciousness of doing

good, peace of mind, and right hope of a glorious destiny hereafter? Away with the word in such a view, and with such a thought! It is emphatically no sacrifice. Say rather it is a privilege. Anxiety, sickness, suffering, or danger, now and then, with a foregoing of the common conveniences and charities of this life, may make us pause, and cause the spirit to waver, and the soul to sink; but let this only be for a moment. All these are nothing when compared with the glory which shall hereafter be revealed in us and for us. I NEVER MADE A SACRIFICE.[280] (emphasis added)

I hold the same view as people often ask me, "Do you miss medicine?", expecting me to start a pity party. I *LOVE* the life the Lord has presently called me to. I was supposed to be dead on July 21, 2008, remember? Really, whether it's leaving the laurels and lucre of medicine and the United Nations or kith and kin in Ghana I dare say, like Livingstone, "I never made a sacrifice."

To think that what I've been called by God to do is statistically sensible, Scripturally sound, stunningly simple, strategically smart, and that *everything* I do has eternal ramifications, *thank you Lord*!

Like the late veteran missionary William Borden, I too have "no reserves," "no retreats," and "no regrets." I only ask for grace to keep *thinking outside the window,* heading where God is going next.

"Never pity missionaries; envy them.
They are where the real action is—
where life and death, sin and grace, Heaven and Hell converge."
~ROBERT C. SHANNON

EPILOGUE

THE ABNORMAL IS THE NEW NORMAL

When I began this book by describing this *African* medical doctor pastoring an *English*-speaking *Chinese* church in a *French* city in North *America,* what I failed to add was that he also serves on the board of *Jews* for Jesus in Canada and has a *Filipino* nanny taking care of his *Ghanaian-Quebecois-Canadian* children in the same home where he hosts a *Pakistani* couple interning with ISMC! Just in case you were thinking all of this was *that* special, let me get you to *think outside the window* again, because that is the current reality of our globalized world of scattered people. This is the new normal.

If I were to describe each of my fellow Table 23 members at a recent Lausanne Global Diaspora Forum in Manila, you will again see how the 'abnormal' has become the norm. Alan, for example, is an *Asian-American* who did his PhD on *Latin America* in *England.* Sitting between him and me (separated by Dr. Moon who works with the diaspora in Korea) was this *German*-speaking *Brazilian* now pastoring an international church in *Kuwait.* Need I go on?...

God is on the move. Moving people around like never before. There are more people on the move in the world now than ever before in the history of mankind. In fact, it is said that should the over 230 million migrants in the world today be considered as a "country," this Global Diaspora would be the fifth largest nation in the world after China, India, the United States and Indonesia!

This is not the same world Abraham migrated across or Jesus was incarnated into or Paul preached to or Constantine Christianized or Martin Luther reformed or even Billy Graham evangelized. "Each generation must... discover its mission, fulfill it or betray it." (Franz Fannon)

As individuals, families, local communities, churches, organizations, academic institutions, corporations, nations, etc. if we do not quickly recognize, study and face the current realities of globalization, diaspora, urbanization, pluralism etc. and *think outside the window* so we snap out of our 19th and 20th Century mindsets and habits, we are in trouble, deep trouble. Worse still, we will not become effective tools in God's hands for what He would have us do for creation and His glory in our nations and generation.

I have shared a bit of my *thinking outside the window* journey with you in the hope that it will encourage you to also do the same and put your hand in the Hand of the Master. You and I don't just want to read and hear about what God did before; we want to be in on the action where He is going *next*.

God is on the move right now! Today is the greatest time to be alive! Get out of your box now!

ACKNOWLEDGMENTS

T hank God for being *my* God—*every good and perfect gift* in and about this book is from Him.

A book like this can obviously never be a solo effort. I am indebted to so many people that I'm afraid beginning to list folks by name may be too dangerous, as I may end up skipping an important name or two, but not out of malice.

I want to thank my dear wife Anyele, who this book is dedicated to, for being the best wife a crazy young man like me could ever have and the best mom our children could've asked God for.

My children make a lot of sacrifices in order to share their dad with the world, and I want to thank Nana Agyina, Nana Ashede, Nana Adwenepa, and Nana Ahotew for their patience with me and for spoiling me with a variety of hugs (including "Turbo" hug, "Puss in Boots" hug, "Kung Fu Panda" hug) and kisses whenever I'm home!

I sincerely thank my fathers, Reindorf Baah Perbi and Nii Kwaku Sowa; my mothers, Akosua Adoma Perbi and Norah Adei Sowa; and all my siblings (Awuraa Amma and Franklin, Paa Nii and Maana, Nana Konadu, Nii Ako, Nana Nketia and Eugenia), cousins and super uncles and aunties (especially "Grandma Rev!") for bearing with the craziness of Anyele and me!

My grandfather is ninety-four years old and doesn't cease to amaze me with his boundless energy, lucid mind, and creativity. A world renowned ethnomusicologist and overachiever, he still makes time to read my books and is always encouraging me in my pursuits. Grandpa, *mo! Nyame nhyira wo!*

Thank you to my Legon Interdenominational Church, Akuapem Ridge Interdenominational Church, ICGC Eagles Temple, Peoples Church of Montreal and Montreal Chinese Alliance Grace Church families for being a spiritual, moral, and financial support to my calling. I owe all my pastors around the world, past and present, a debt of gratitude, especially Dr. Mensa Otabil, Very Rev. Prof. Kwabena Asamoah-Gyadu, Rev. Dr. Maxwell Aryee, Rev. Prof. John Azumah, Rev. Yaw Boamah, Rev. Agnes Phillips, Rev. Frank Humphrey, Ps. Bryan Guinness, and Rev. Philip Cherng.

I am grateful to God for my longstanding mentors, Dr. Mensa Otabil, Uncle Ebo Whyte and Ken Ofori-Atta.

Thank you to my Scripture Union, IFES (especially GHAFES), Navigators and Excellent Youth Outreach (EYO) families for the grounding in God's *Word,* enabling me to catch a vision for God's *world* and *work.*

I owe my teachers, from Ridge Church School through Achimota to the University of Ghana Medical School, tons of gratitude.

Thank you to all my commanding and senior officers, colleagues and staff of the 37 Military Hospital in Accra for the privilege of working alongside you. I owe a special debt of gratitude to my UNOCI Ghanmed 5 team in Bouake, Côte d'Ivoire—they were a bulwark of strength during our one year together, especially around the time of the fatal accident. Special thanks to my commanding officer Colonel Adjei. Although departed, I want to say thank you to Maj. (Dr.) Archer and Staff Sergeant Dogbevia for laying down their lives in the course of duty, as we served together.

When we first arrived in Canada, Jessica, Sacha, and Dino gave us their apartment to stay in because they were yet to move in. Thank you! We all had *no idea* the *big* plans God had in store, but you willingly offered your manger.

I owe a debt of gratitude to all my founding members of The HuD Group as well as past and current leaders (board and executive alike) the world over who have graciously borne with me as I seemed to have 'abandoned ship' to captain ISMC. It's *all* God's kingdom; not ours or about us!

Without my ISMC family, this book wouldn't exist. I want to thank every single one of my 110 staff from *sea to shining sea* (many times when I travel I don't even need to stay in a hotel!). I want to especially thank my board and the national leadership team, which miraculously runs ISMC from and across nine different provinces in Canada! To Keith, Twylla, Barbara, Winona, Cam and Syncia in particular, thank you for standing by me and with me to pursue our big, hairy, audacious God-sized Vision 2020+. ISMC folks, "I am because you are."

I want to single out Paul Workentine at ISMC, my predecessor. His show of selfless leadership, stepping aside, and inviting me to take his seat is rare, even in Christendom, in this day and age. Thank you, Paul and Ruth, for your selfless service. They not only invited me to come on board, they almost always host me in their home whenever I'm in Calgary, and still work with me in the ministry!

Our sister-ministry in the United States (or should I say mother-ministry, since they birthed ISMC over thirty years ago), International Students Inc., has been such an encouragement and ready resource to ISMC in general and me in particular. I want to extend very warm thanks to Doug Shaw, the president, and the entire leadership and membership of ISI. Blessings, guys! I had a great time with you in Colorado Springs. We're in this together *forever!*

As I thank God for the Lausanne family, I would like to single out board chair Doug Birdsall for not only leading Lausanne as a whole to afford me the experiences I've had, but for taking a personal interest in me, including calling me on the phone from time to time! Thank you Doug. To Papa Jim Chew, and my fellow group members who haven't stopped encouraging me since YLG '06, *medaase*. Thank you Michael Oh, current Lausanne Executive Director, for your friendship since YLG '06.

My bosom friend, Nana Yaw Offei-Awuku, and his wife Beth have walked with me and grown alongside me as peers in perceiving and responding to God's global call from our African context *together.* Thank you.

What a privilege I've had pastoring the Montreal Chinese Alliance Grace Church. Thank you for the opportunity, Rev. Cherng. O such love I have for you all, my congregants! I owe special thanks to my leadership team because without them—Caleb, George, Leon, Lisa, Zoe, Lian, Ran, Sam, James, Ming-Te, Isaac, Ying, Edward—there is no way I could ever have managed pastoring a growing church and leading a sprawling mission like ISMC.

Since taking on full-time, career-missionary status, we have totally depended on the prayer and financial contributions of scores of family and friends and churches around the world, especially in Ghana, Canada, and the United States. Although I may not be able to list all your names here, God knows your name and He will repay you.

My siblings Awuraa Amma and Franklin (my best male friend) have in particular been indispensable in mobilizing the Body of Christ in Ghana to see the strategic vision and mission of ISMC and tap into it. Without their encouragement, prayers, logistical arrangements, and direct financial support, there are whole chapters of this book that wouldn't exist—we wouldn't even be talking about "Money from Africa." Thank you, guys! Anyele and I love you so much!

Merci beaucoup Paul Borthwick, ever-busy and in such high demand globally, for graciously agreeing to write the foreword. Thanks Leiton Chinn for the introduction—I owe you and the entire founding membership of the Lausanne International Student Ministries Global Leadership Network big time—Terry (New Zealand), Emma (South Africa), and Richard (UK).

Thank you to all my friends who endorsed this book—J.D., Femi, Philip, Nana Yaw, Beau and Bradley.

Thank you Carmen Bryant, Beau Miller, and the entire ACMI (Association of Christians Ministering among Internationals) family for the warm hand of fellowship.

Many friends have encouraged me to complete this book. Some of them like Kingsley (and Afua) and Sammy (and Gifty), have been international students themselves, and having participated in God's new wave of missions from the Global South, have longed for this day when some of these experiences will be documented and shared. Well, now you have it. Thank you for encouraging me to press on!

I want to thank the teeming international students who give us the opportunity to love and lead them. What a joy and privilege to literally serve the world at our doorstep! There will be no ISMC without y'all. Thank you in particular to those like Kenji, Sangeeta, Clement, Julie, Isaac and Manuel who gladly allow me to share their stories with the world.

Finally, to Loretta Zwaan (my reliable virtual assistant), Angie (my brilliant cover designer) and the entire Xulon team, you've been fun, professional and phenomenal. Let's do this again!

TO LEARN MORE

If you are inspired and touched by *Thinking Outside the Window* to commit to making a difference in the world with your life, empowering international students to impact the world through Jesus Christ, the book's website will be a great way to start.

On the site you will find:

- tangible things you can do to make a difference for international students
- a place to share your own stories and experiences with others on the same journey
- more stories of people here and around the world whose lives have been changed because they got involved
- the "Thinking Outside the Window" forum, where you can join with others in a dialogue on changing the world through international students
- links to other resources, articles, websites, and statistics
- resources for churches who want to get involved in a deeper way
- videos that show what's being done in Canada and around the world to empower international students to impact the world
- stories of international alumni and the impact they are making in the world today

Go to <u>www.thinkingoutsidethewindow.com</u>

ISMC

INTERNATIONAL STUDENT
MINISTRIES CANADA

WHO WE ARE

ISMC is an interdenominational faith mission incorporated in Canada and supported by friends who share our vision to "empower international students to impact the world through Jesus Christ."

HOW WE SERVE

- Linking students with Canadian friendship partners
- Hosting international dinners and special events
- Offering Bible studies to students interested in learning about Christianity
- Praying for international students
- Making ESL classes available
- Offering airport pickup
- Training internationals for godly, effectual leadership

WHERE WE SERVE

From coast to coast in *British Columbia* (Victoria, Vancouver, Prince George, Abbotsford, Kamloops, Kelowna), *Alberta* (Calgary, Edmonton, Three Hills), *Saskatchewan* (Regina, Saskatoon), *Manitoba* (Brandon, Winnipeg),

Ontario (Thunder Bay, Sault Ste. Marie, London, St. Catharine's, Waterloo, Guelph, Hamilton, Greater Toronto Area, Peterborough, Ottawa), *Quebec* (Montreal, Sherbrooke), *New Brunswick* (Fredericton, Moncton), and *Nova Scotia* (Halifax).

Go to **www.ismc.ca** for more information

THINKING OUTSIDE THE WINDOW
STUDY GUIDE

PART I
WHAT BOX? WHOSE BOX?

Go to www.thinkingoutsidethewindow.com

PART II
EVEN THE HEAVENS CAN'T; LET ALONE YOUR BOX

Go to www.thinkingoutsidethewindow.com

PART III
DON'T GET BOXED IN

Go to www.thinkingoutsidethewindow.com

ENDNOTES

1   http://en.wikipedia.org/wiki/Thinking_outside_the_box

2   https://airandspace.si.edu/exhibitions/wright-brothers/online/fly/1903/ (accessed 10 November, 2014)

3   http://www.achievement.org/achievers/ban0/text/ban0pro.html (accessed 10 November 2014)

4   *Encyclopaedia Britannica,* http://www.britannica.com/EBchecked/topic/385426/mission (last retrieved on 27 January, 2015)

5   Jesus Christ, Matthew 6:22–23

6   http://joshuaproject.net/countries/IN (accessed 13 March, 2015)

7   http://joshuaproject.net/global_statistics (accessed 10 November, 2014)

8   http://joshuaproject.net/resources/articles/has_everyone_heard (accessed 10 November, 2014)

9   http://joshuaproject.net/global_statistics (accessed 10 November, 2014)

10 http://joshuaproject.net/resources/articles/has_everyone_heard (accessed 10 November, 2014)

11 Ibid.

12 Zwemer, Samuel M. *The Unoccupied Mission Fields of Africa and Asia.* (New York: Student Volunteer Movement for Foreign Missions, 1911), 260.

13 http://en.wikipedia.org/wiki/10/40_Window

14 1 John 1:1. Luke's careful research (Luke 1:3) was a classic exception.

15   Reported in the Lausanne Movement's *Connecting Point ENewsletter* of 27 July, 2011 and other Lausanne Movement media (http://mye-mail.constantcontact.com/Lausanne-Connecting-Point—-June—-July-2011.html?soid=1011244526119&aid=A-bnRHSJDqo)

16   http://www.ecumenicalnews.com/article/shift-of-center-of-chris-tian-gravity-to-global-south-most-dramatic-in-history-22528

17   Preamble, *The Cape Town Commitment, A confession of Faith and a Call to Action,* AcadSA Publishing, Panorama, Parow, South Africa, Africa Edition, 2012, pg. 7.

18   http://www.ecumenicalnews.com/article/shift-of-center-of-chris-tian-gravity-to-global-south-most-dramatic-in-history-22528

19   Ibid.

20   Jason Mandryk. *Operation World: The Definitive Prayer Guide to Every Nation, 7ᵗʰ ed.,* (Colorado Springs: Biblica Publishing, 2010), 949.

21   Ibid, 951.

22   Gerrie ter Haar, "African Christians in the Netherlands," in *Religious Communities in the Diaspora*, ed. Gerrie ter Haar (Nairobi, Kenya: Acton Publishers, 2001), 166.

23   In actuality, all my children except the first are Quebec-born.

24   Romans 10:12

25   Acts 10:34–35, English Standard Version (ESV). Also referenced the King James Version (KJV) and New International Version (NIV) for verse 34.

26   Genesis 12:1

27   In the Ghana Armed Forces, a Group Captain in the Air Force is the equivalent of Colonel in the army.

28   Luke 23:43

29   2 Corinthians 6:2, New Living Translation

30   John 9:4

31   John 6:29

32   Galatians 2:20

33 This is not to say medicine is not or cannot be ministry; I speak of ministry here as "pulpit ministry" and "youth ministry."

34 Psalm 18:30a

35 "Akwaaba" means "welcome" in the Akan language of Ghana, my mother tongue.

36 http://www.pioneers-africa.org/content/how-it-began (last accessed 15 January, 2015)

37 Jeremiah 1:5, New Living Translation

38 Psalm 18:30a

39 Paul Borthwick, *Western Christians in Global Mission: what's the role of the North American church?,* Intervarsity Press, Downers Grove, Illinois, 2012, 45.

40 Ibid.

41 Isaiah 46:10

42 Just about when I was finishing this book I unexpectedly got a call from the new Executive Director of ACMI (Association of Christians Ministry among Internationals), inviting me to be a plenary speaker at the next ACMI conference in 2015 at Wheaton College, near Chicago (USA). Guess the theme of the conference? "ISM: The Next Chapter in Missions History."

43 Isaiah 41:2

44 Genesis 1:1–2, New American Standard Bible

45 Genesis 12:1

46 Acts 17:26

47 Acts 17:27

48 Acts 1:8; Matthew 28:18-20

49 Acts 8:4

50 http://esa.un.org/unmigration/wallchart2013.htm (accessed 02 October, 2014)

51 Ibid.

52 Ibid.

53 Ibid.

54   Calculated using the above information and 2013 population figures of these same countries.

55   *http://www.unhcr.org/53a155bc6.html* (accessed 08 November, 2014)

56   Ibid.

57   Even in reading the history of West Africa, where I hail from, it has been interesting to note that there were international students from my region of the world from as far back as the eighteenth century, with the likes of Anton Wilhem Amo, Jacobus Capitein, and Philip Quaque. Robert W. July asserts that early international student trailblazers like these three actually "initiated a pattern which became common in the nineteenth century by going to Europe for early training." *The Origins of African Modern Thought: its development in West Africa during the nineteenth and twentieth centuries,* Africa World Press, 2004, 34.

58   http://www.oecd.org/edu/Education-at-a-Glance-2014.pdf, p. 344

59   http://www.oecd.org/edu/Education-at-a-Glance-2014.pdf, p. 343

60   http://www.cbie.ca/about-ie/facts-and-figures/ (OECD projections, accessed 10 December, 2014)

61   http://www.oecd.org/edu/Education-at-a-Glance-2014.pdf, p. 344 (accessed 08 November, 2014)

62   Ibid.

63   Ibid.

64   http://www.oecd.org/edu/Education-at-a-Glance-2014.pdf, p. 351 (from chart C.4.5)

65   Organization for Economic Co-operation and Development, founded in 1961 and with thirty-four members, but in practicality brings around its table forty countries that account for 80 percent of world trade and investment. (http://www.oecd.org/about/history/)

66   http://www.oecd.org/edu/Education-at-a-Glance-2014.pdf, p. 344 (accessed 08 November, 2014).

67   Ibid.

68   Ibid.

69   Ibid.

70   Ibid.

71   http://www.immigrationwatchcanada.org (last accessed March
      13, 2015)

72   Ibid.

73   Ibid.

74   Colin Hansen's correspondence with Ps. John Mahaffey, senior pastor
      of West Highland Baptist Church in Hamilton, Ontario (http://
      www.thegospelcoalition.org/article/the-state-of-the-church-in-
      canada (last accessed 21 January, 2015).

75   Ibid.

76   In absolute terms, this northern neighbor of the United States is even
      more significant than that per capita. (In absolute terms, the United
      States hosted most of these students, with 16 percent of all foreign
      students, followed by the United Kingdom (13 percent), Germany (6
      percent), France (6 percent), Australia (6 percent) and Canada (5 per-
      cent). (http://www.oecd.org/edu/Education-at-a-Glance-2014.pdf,
      p. 344 (accessed 08 November, 2014)

77   http://monitor.icef.com/2014/11/record-high-internation-
      al-enrolment-canada-2013-many-students-plan-stay (accessed 25
      November, 2014)

78   My paraphrase of Isaiah 55:8-9

79   Ibid.

80   Ibid.

81   https://www.grad.ubc.ca/prospective-students/international-stu-
      dents (accessed January 12, 2015)

82   http://www.oecd.org/edu/Education-at-a-Glance-2014.pdf, Pg. 344
      (accessed 08 November, 2014)

83   http://en.wikipedia.org/wiki/Fort_St._John,_British_Columbia
      (accessed 22 October, 2014)

84   Ibid.

85 http://www.westjet.com/vacations/en/destinations/destina-
    tion-overview.shtml?id=DBRIYXJ (accessed October 22, 2014)
86 http://www.westjet.com/guest/en/deals/offers/summer-schedule.
    shtml (accessed October 22, 2014)
87 John 4:35–38
88 Numbers 22:21–35
89 Numbers 22:31
90 Luke 24:31–32
91 John 4:31–34
92 http://fortune.com/2014/07/14/us-canada-economy/ (last accessed
    12 January 2015)
93 John 4:9
94 An Issachar Initiative that ISMC and my church, as well as many
    others have bought into (see http://www.issacharinitiative.org/
    count-for-zero/)
95 http://canadaboundimmigrant.com/education/article.php?id=498
    (accessed 15 November, 2014)
96 Ibid.
97 Ephesians 3:20, King James Version
98 http://monitor.icef.com/2014/11/record-high-internation-
    al-enrolment-canada-2013-many-students-plan-stay (accessed 25
    November, 2014)
99 http://news.gc.ca/web/article-en.do?nid=722709 (original accessed
    in June 2013 but archived version accessed 25 November, 2014)
100 http://www.cic.gc.ca/english/resources/statistics/facts2013-prelimi-
    nary/07.asp (accessed 18 December, 2014)
101 http://www.cbie.ca/news/cbie-launches-status-report-on-na-
    tions-performance-in-international-education/ (accessed 28
    November, 2014)
102 Ibid.
103 http://www.utoronto.ca/about-uoft/quickfacts

104 http://engineering.ubc.ca/sites/apsc.ubc.ca/files/ubcengineering_
undergraduate_viewbook.pdf (accessed January 12, 2015)

105 https://www.grad.ubc.ca/prospective-students/international-stu-
dents (accessed January 12, 2015)

106 http://monitor.icef.com/2015/01/national-survey-shows-cana-
dian-universities-focused-internationalisation/ (last accessed 25
January, 2015)

107 http://monitor.icef.com/2014/11/record-high-internation-
al-enrolment-canada-2013-many-students-plan-stay (accessed 25
November, 2014)

108 Ibid.

109 Tamara Baluja, The Globe and Mail, Aug 14, 2012 (http://www.can-
adaka.net/link.php?id=76096)

110 http://metronews.ca/news/calgary/609007/university-of-cal-
gary-aims-to-double-international-student-enrolment-ex-
change-programs/

111 www.universityworldnews.com/article.
php?story=20120819074703508

112 Tamara Baluja, The Globe and Mail, Aug 14, 2012 (http://www.can-
adaka.net/link.php?id=76096)

113 http://news.gc.ca/web/article-en.do?nid=722709 (original accessed
in June 2013 but archived version accessed 25 November, 2014)

114 Tamara Baluja, The Globe and Mail, Aug 14, 2012 (http://www.can-
adaka.net/link.php?id=76096)

115 http://www.vancouversun.com/business/
Opinion+International+students+vital/8969776/story.html
(accessed 10 August, 2013)

116 www.universityworldnews.com/article.
php?story=20120819074703508

117 Ibid.

118 http://www.thestar.com/yourtoronto/education/2014/09/11/
international_students_or_cash_cows.html (last accessed October
25, 2014)

119 http://www.vancouversun.com/business/
Opinion+International+students+vital/8969776/story.html
(accessed 10 August, 2013)

120 Martin Randall is the executive director of the British Columbia
Council for International Education (BCCIE).

121 http://www.vancouversun.com/business/
Opinion+International+students+vital/8969776/story.html
(accessed 10 August, 2013)

122 http://finance.yahoo.com/news/canada-welcomes-record-num-
ber-international-140000011.html

123 Mark 16:15 (also Matthew 28:18-20)

124 Acts 2:5–11, New Living Translation

125 Matthew 25:31–35; 37–38; 40

126 James 2:8; Leviticus 19:18

127 Leviticus 19:34

128 Hebrews 13:2

129 Ibid, English Standard Version

130 Leviticus 19:34

131 Ibid.

132 Leviticus 19:33, New Living Translation

133 Ibid, NIV.

134 *http://www.thestar.com/yourtoronto/education/2014/09/11/interna-
tional_students_or_cash_cows.html* (last accessed October 25, 2014)

135 Ibid.

136 Ibid.

137 http://www.bbc.co.uk/worldservice/specials/1458_abolition/
page4.shtml

138 http://www.globalslaveryindex.org/findings/

139 Ephesians 2:12

140 http://www.cbc.ca/news/canada/montreal/
head-found-in-montreal-park-belongs-to-jun-lin-1.1229810

141 http://www.ctvnews.ca/canada/magnotta-found-guilty-of-first-de-
gree-murder-1.2159607#ixzz30SIALi2s

142 http://www.cbc.ca/news/canada/montreal/
head-found-in-montreal-park-belongs-to-jun-lin-1.1229810

143 http://www.ctvnews.ca/canada/
magnotta-found-guilty-of-first-degree-murder-1.2159607

144 Ibid.

145 http://www.ctvnews.ca/canada/magnotta-found-guilty-of-first-de-
gree-murder-1.2159607#ixzz30SGqwMEs

146 Genesis 50:20a, God's Word Translation

147 http://www.torontosun.com/2014/12/29/jun-lins-father-says-no-
forgiveness-for-magnotta (accessed 12 January, 2014)

148 Ibid.

149 Ibid.

150 Ibid.

151 John Cudderford, January 8 2015 Newsletter, Vol. 3 No. 10, p. 1

152 Agbeti, John Kofi. 1986. *West African Church History: Christian
Missions and Church Foundations, 1482-1919.* (Leiden, Netherlands:
E.J. Brill.)

153 Jeremiah 29:13, New Living Translation

154 *"A brief history of the Wesleyan missions on the west coast of Africa:
including biographical sketches of all the missionaries who have died in
that important field of labour : with some account of the European set-
tlements and of the slave-trade"* by William Fox, January 1, 1851 (digi-
talized by Google, accessed via Google reader on December 27, 2014)

155 Essamuah, Casely . *Genuinely Ghanaian: A History of the Methodist
Church Ghana, 1961-2000,* Africa World Press, Inc. 2010, 11. In
combination with William Fox's book, cited in note 154 above.

156 See Leviticus 16.

157 Isaiah 5:1–4

158   Malachi 3:6, King James Version

159   Isaiah 55:8–9, New Living Translation

160   Computation done by consultant Terry Mochar and his research team based on CIA facts and other sources, in ISMC's Ministry Effectiveness Project document, 2011.

161   Lailani herself was an international from the Philippines, greatly benefited from our ministry, and is now serving with us as Associate Staff in Edmonton.

162   Mendoza, Lailani Ed. *Touches of the Master's Hand: Changing Lives— Impacting the World.* (ISMC, 2009), 38.

163   FOCUS—Fellowship of Overseas College & University Students/ Friendship for Overseas College & University Students, organized by ISMC in almost every major city in Canada, usually in collaboration with local churches.

164   All the indented information from http://win1040.com/about-the-1040-window.php (accessed 12 January 2015)

165   This analysis done from 2013 Canadian numbers. See http://monitor.icef.com/2014/11/record-high-international-enrolment-canada-2013-many-students-plan-stay (accessed 25 November, 2014)

166   Isaiah 43:19

167   Romans 15:20

168   See www.issacharinitiative.org

169   Count for Zero Participants Guide, Issachar Initiative 2014, p. 76

170   http://joshuaproject.net/countries/PK

171   An example of the reportage around that time may be found at http://www.theblaze.com/stories/2013/11/12/reports-north-korea-executed-80-people-for-watching-tv-and-owning-bibles/

172   Acts 8:6–8, 12

173   Acts 8:26, English Standard Version (ESV)

174   Acts 8:27a, ESV

175   Acts 8:29, ESV

176   Acts 8:30–31, ESV

177   Acts 8:35, ESV

178   Acts 17:22–23

179   Facts of our conversation were later confirmed by a later Bible Society of Ghana press release (see http://www.ghanaweb.com/GhanaHomePage/regional/artikel.php?ID=90783)

180   Ibid.

181   Ibid.

182   Romans 8:18–22

183   A fuller version of this "3D" can be found in another work by the author. This is just a summary of the big ideas.

184   Psalm 82:1–8

185   Revelation 12:1-5

186   Coleman, Robert E. *The Master Plan of Evangelism*. (Grand Rapids, MI: Revell, 1972 [with study guide]), 31-32.

187   See http://www.brotherbakhtsingh.com/

188   http://mastercardfdnscholars.org/about/

189   http://news.ubc.ca/2013/04/18/25m-gift-brings-african-students-to-ubc/

190   2 Corinthians 3:2–3

191   Hastings, Adrian. *The Church in Africa 1450-1950*. (Oxford, UK: Clarendon Press. 1994), 178.

192   Luke 6:13

193   1 Samuel 16

194   2 Timothy 2:2 in the English Standard Version, King James Version or North American Standard Bible have the word "faithful" as the criterion for those to be trained while others like the NIV use "reliable."

195   Matthew 4:19

196   Coleman, 22.

197   Acts 17:6

198   Mark 3:14a

199   Acts 4:13

200   Coleman, 33.

201 Luke 10:1

202 The aim of this project was to be able to raise money for brilliant but needy tertiary students in the developing world, in places where Compassion Canada operates.

203 Several places in scripture. In Matthew 5 alone, see verses 27–28, 31–32, 33–34, 38–39, 43–44

204 Weaver, Richard M. *Ideas Have Consequences*. (Chicago, IL: University of Chicago Press. 1948).

205 Marshall, Paul A. *Stained Glass: Worldviews and Social Science* (Lanham, MD: University Press of America. 1989), 8.

206 Romans 12:2

207 John 20:21b, English Standard Version

208 S-H-A-P-E as learnt from Rick Warren—Spiritual gifts, Heartfelt passions, Abilities, Personality, Experiences

209 John 3:3 and several places in the New Testament

210 Matthew 28:18–20, The Message

211 Colossians 2:8

212 Joshua 1:8

213 Mark 13:31

214 Matthew 5:13

215 A simple way all of us participants at the Third Lausanne Congress on World Evangelization in Cape Town (2010) were exhorted to live like Christ and go and share this message with the rest of the global church.

216 http://www.worldbank.org/en/news/speech/2013/01/30/world-bank-group-president-jim-yong-kim-speech-anti-corruption-center-for-strategic-and-international-studies (last accessed January 15, 2015)

217 Luke 2:52

218 Acts 1:8

219 1 John 1:1, New Living Translation

220 Matthew 28:18

221 Acts 10:38, New Living Translation

222 Luke 11:1

223 See www.thehudgroup.ca or www.thehudgroup.org

224 Coleman, 32.

225 Brilliant quote picked up from Betty Barnett's amazing book, *Friend Raising*, attributed to Bonnie C. Bishop's article, "Asking for Money," *World Christian Magazine*, 1986, Nov./Dec., 28

226 Romans 10:15, English Standard Version

227 Psalm 121:1–2

228 An application of Romans 12:2

229 http://bhehrmissions.blogspot.ca/2010/02/series-on-support-raising. html (accessed 03 January, 2015)

230 Barnett Betty. *Friend Raising*, (Seattle, WA: YWAM publishing. 1991), 13.

231 Ibid.

232 Barnett, 37.

233 Ibid.

234 Ibid.

235 Barnett, 38.

236 Ibid.

237 Mark 8:37

238 Barnett, 38.

239 Barnett, 40

240 Nouwen, Henri. *The Spirituality of Fundraising*, Estate of Henri J.M. Nouwen, 2004.

241 Barnett, 40

242 Ibid.

243 Ibid.

244 Nouwen, iv

245 Ibid.

246 Ibid., iv-v.

247 Carter, Doug, *Raising More than Money*, Thomas Nelson, Nashville, Tennessee 2007, IX.

248 L.O.V.E. (Listen to them, Open your heart to them, Value them, Exemplify generosity); L.E.A.D. (Lay out the dream, Explain the strategy, Ask them for partnership, Deliver what you promise); L.I.N.K. (Lift them up in prayer, Involve them, Never take them for granted, Keep them informed); L.I.F.T. (Listen to them, Invest in them, Facilitate their dreams, Thank them often). Ibid, 103 (Figure 10.1 of EQUIP's Relational Funding Model).

249 Ibid.

250 Matthew 10:41a, New Living Translation

251 1 Corinthians 9:7a

252 Luke 8:1–3

253 http://bhehrmissions.blogspot.ca/2010/02/series-on-support-raising.html (accessed 03 January, 2015)

254 Business as Mission Lausanne Occasional Paper No. 59. Produced by the issue group on this topic at the 2004 Forum for World Evangelization hosted by the Lausanne Committee for World Evangelization in Pattaya, Thailand, September 29 to October 5, 2004, pg. 9 (introduction)

255 1989 Manila Congress (The Second Lausanne Congress) definition of tentmakers.

256 These "revelations" about William Carey came to me only recently, after receiving a *Tentmakers International* (TI) monthly newsletter from my friend Johnny Chun (executive director of TI) on 3 January, 2014. We were at the World Evangelical Alliance Mission Commission consultation in Izmir together, a few months before (in May 2014).

257 http://www.economist.com/blogs/baobab/2014/04/remittances-africa (accessed 19 September , 2014)

258 2 Kings 7

259 Aldridge John, "The Lions Roar," *The Sunday Times Magazine* 26.2.2012, 45.

260 Ibid.

261 Ibid.

262 Africa's Wealthy Give back, UBS and Trust Africa, 1.

263 Ibid., 2

264 An October 1, 2014 email from Nana Yaw Offei-Awuku to me in response to my request to send the latest version of his write-up on the evolving Missions Africa Trust Fund. The attachment, from which I quote, was actually an impending global press-release statement.

265 Ibid.

266 http://www.economist.com/blogs/baobab/2014/04/remittances-africa (accessed 19 September , 2014)

267 Ralph Winter, "Reconsecration to a Wartime, Not a Peacetime, Lifestyle," in *Perspectives on the World Christian Movement,* 3rd ed., ed. Ralph Winter and Steven Hawthorne (Pasadena, Calif.: William Carey. 1999), 705.

268 Luke 21:3-4, Msg.

269 http://www.biblesociety.org.uk/about-bible-society/our-work/mary-jones/ (accessed 30 September, 2014)

270 http://www.unitedbiblesocieties.org/ (accessed 30 September, 2014)

271 Aldridge John, "The Lions Roar," *The Sunday Times Magazine* 26.2.2012, 49.

272 Galatians 2:20

273 Proverbs 16:7, English Standard Version

274 Luke 9:62

275 Final test that concludes the first year or two of course work; passing it is a prerequisite to continue in the program; failing means, being sacked or asked to withdraw.

276 See http://digital.faithtoday.ca/faithtoday/20130708?pg=8#pg8 (last checked on 28 January, 2015)

277 Acts 4:12

278 2 Samuel 7:18

279 Isaiah 55:8–9, New Living Translation

280 Cited in Samuel Zwemer, "The Glory of the Impossible," *Perspectives on the World Christian Movement*, 4th ed., ed. Ralph D. Winter and Stephen C. Hawthorne (Pasadena, Calif.: William Carey, 2009), 333.